Recovery Beyond Psychiatry

David Whitwell
January 2005

Published in the United Kingdom 2005
by Free Association Books
London

British Library Cataloguing in Publication Data
A catalogue record for this book is available from the British Library

Produced by Bookchase, London
Printed and bound in the EU

ISBN 1853439231

Dedication

"for my family – Carolyn, Thomas, Susie and Imogen;
and also Katherine and my dear lamented brother Richard."

David Whitwell
davidwhitwell@blueyonder.co.uk

Contents

Introduction   i

PART I THE MYTH THAT PSYCHIATRIC TREATMENT PRODUCES RECOVERY   1

Chapter 1 The Origins of Naïve Psychiatry   2

Chapter 2 Asking Psychiatrists and their Patients About Recovery   22

Chapter 3 The Challenge to the Medical Model   26

Chapter 4 The Endless Debate   36

Chapter 5 Narratives and Human Existence   50

Chapter 6 The Reactions of the Self to Mental Illness   60

PART II THE REALITY OF PERSONAL SURVIVAL AND RECOVERY   75

Chapter 7 Evidence of Recovery   76

Chapter 8 The Long Road to Recovery   89

Chapter 9 Naturalistic Factors in Recovery   93

Chapter 10 False Solutions   108

Chapter 11 Treatment, Therapy and Recovery   112

Chapter 12 Drug Treatment in Psychiatry   122

Chapter 13 The Human Factor   149

Chapter 14 Survival of the Personal Life   158

Chapter 15 Regaining Control   170

Chapter 16 New Services: New Model.   181

Acknowledgements   188
References   189

Introduction:

RECOVERY FROM MENTAL ILLNESS

If you can understand how people recover from mental illness, then you may be able to help them. This was my starting point. After being a psychiatrist for many years, I had come to realise that psychiatry is all about symptoms and illness and has little to say about recovery. What it does say is quite naïve and simple, just that if you have the right treatment you ought to recover; that vigorous treatment can make people recover. In my early days as a hospital psychiatrist this seemed to work: people would be admitted in a desperate and disturbed state and go home much improved. The treatments seemed to produce recovery, just as was claimed. However as I got to know my patients better, I was not so sure. Psychiatric treatment could certainly remove symptoms, but had the people really recovered? I began to talk to more and more people about this, and found that there are widely differing ideas about what recovery is, and little agreement about how it should be achieved. Traditionally, psychiatry focuses on "clinical recovery" which involves losing symptoms and regaining normal function, whereas for others, especially those who have been through the system, recovery is much more than this. The Recovery Movement (Robert & Wolfson 2004) focuses on rebuilding a rewarding and meaningful personal life, something that has been overlooked by psychiatric research.

As a practising general psychiatrist I found that many of my patients were not making good recoveries, when this was judged in narrow clinical terms. I began to ask about recovery and listen to people's personal accounts. It was clear that they thought they were not achieving this elusive thing called recovery. This was depressing. All that treatment and intervention in people's lives, aimed at making them recover, but in the end leaving many thinking that they had failed. If recovery could be defined in more personal and meaningful terms, I was not sure we were even looking for it. I concluded that the recovery promised by medical treatment is a myth; held out as a goal, but rarely attainable. I wrote a short paper about this called "The Myth of Recovery from Mental Illness"(Whitwell 1999), and upset a lot of people who thought I was being negative and unhelpful, casting doubt on their hopes for recovery. I can see their point and I apologise for that. My quarrel is with the idea that *treatment* can make people recover, not with the idea that *people* can recover. I think there is a very positive message about recovery; it is possible and attainable, but depends on the active involvement of the individual. I am not an anti-psychiatrist but think that psychiatry needs to be kept in its place. It can do great things to support people, keep them alive, and alleviate their complaints, but it cannot give them a new life.

The myth that treatment makes people recover is a medical myth and is at the centre of "naïve psychiatry". It forms the basic approach still underlying much work in mental health, even though most psychiatrists would disown it. One of the odd things about psychiatry is that totally different levels of discourse can coexist. A rarefied level of complicated theories about people and their motivations exists, as abstract and remote from reality as the higher realms of philosophy. These theories are difficult and abstruse and take many years to master. Those who have mastered them enjoy endless discussions about how particular patients' conditions may be explained. At a much lower level, street level, are pragmatic theories about how to deal with people in the day to day management of the mental health service. These, by contrast, can be crude and dehumanising in the extreme. Most books are written about the clever theories - so interesting to study and develop - but the ground level theories (those forming what I call "naïve psychiatry") are the ones that influence how people are treated in practice. It is the concept of recovery, implicit in naïve psychiatry, that I want to challenge.

I have to confess to having practised naïve psychiatry for years, and that this book is a record of my gradual realisation of the inadequacy of this approach. I am laying myself open here, it will be easy for people to say that I have simply got things wrong. I have illustrated my discussion with cases loosely based on people I have treated, and I am afraid they may not present my practice of psychiatry in a very good light. I can only say that I have worked as a busy general psychiatrist for many years and I don't think my experiences are unusual. All psychiatrists have had to find ways to move on from the limited ideas they started with; they each have their own ways to humanise the so-called medical model. For some, the growing awareness of the limitations of what can be done leads to disillusionment. While they have been trying to humanise psychiatry, the opposing forces require psychiatrists to become more like policemen. One thing which follows from the myth that treatment can produce recovery is that the medical professions are expected to deliver it.

In Part I, I look at the way that a rigid concern with being scientific has made it difficult for psychiatry to adopt a more broad and humane model of recovery. There is the question of whether scientific explanations are adequate to describe the personal life of the individual. Science is essential for many things including the management of treatment but all theories are essentially oversimplifications. They separate out small aspects of the person and focus on them because they have some special relevance. They cut through the bewildering complexity of human life to a few aspects that can be studied in detail. However there is no science that can be applied to the person as a whole, and so no substitute for the understanding that comes from looking at the person in the context of the narrative of their life. Science has its place, but so do narratives and personal accounts, and the latter have particular importance for understanding recovery.

The over-preoccupation with science means that research into how people recover focuses almost entirely on the specific treatments for particular conditions advocated by professionals. These include drugs, ECT and psychotherapy. The incidental helpful things that tend to occur whenever any form of help is offered are termed non-specific factors. They include restoring hope, providing emotional and practical support and personal contact. These are also called placebo factors, as they are present in interventions from which the active ingredients have been removed. Naturalistic factors are like non-specific factors in not being prescribed by professionals, but these are things that occur outside treatment, things like life events, new experiences, relationships and the passage of time. These tend to be new, forward-looking factors, whereas treatment and therapy tend to be anchored in the past. I will argue that naturalistic and other non-specific factors play a major part in bringing about recovery, but are ignored by research, and so by professionals.

Non-specific factors rely on types of human interaction that are ancient and universal. They could be encouraged by a system that recognised and valued them, but they get sidelined by our present mental health system. All specific interventions have powerful pressure groups behind them, making exaggerated claims and ensuring that they dominate the field. In the conflict between clever technical interventions and simple human responses to people in distress, it is the clever interventions that are winning. A major concern is that the clever interventions are not as good as is claimed.

One way to highlight this debate is to start from the null hypothesis. What would be the implications if none of the treatments worked? What if not one drug were better than a placebo and none of the therapies better than friendly, supportive conversation? Or maybe they do work, but only for some people? There again, maybe the real benefits are marginal, only detectable by careful statistical analysis. The question is - what would this mean for psychiatry? I am not advocating that this is the case, I'm sure some treatments are useful - but it is a good starting point for discussion. Many of the things that can help people to recover are general non-specific measures, such as, steps to help someone take back control of their own life, and help to protect and develop their personal life. In spite of all the emphasis on specific treatments, it will be claimed in this book that for most people it is non-specific factors that contribute most to recovery.

New models of treatment including Early Intervention and Home Treatment are beginning to move things in this direction. They are quietly ignoring the medical model and working with models of personal recovery, focusing on the individual's aspirations and needs and placing less emphasis on medical treatment. However no service will ever be ideal; there will always be a conflict between individuals and those who administer large public systems. There is an innate bossiness in systems and part of being a helper involves being on the side of the individual against the system.

The conclusion is that recovery should be adopted as the goal of mental health services. Treatment then becomes just one option that can be used in certain situations. Acute psychiatry becomes a particular set of procedures for dealing with urgent and dangerous situations. Its aims are limited. It is a special kind of first aid, which needs to be fitted into the individual's long-term recovery plan. This change will be unwelcome to those who like the idea that having the right treatment will ensure recovery. It is true that people go through phases in which they are not ready to recover. They may need to be sustained and kept alive until they are more settled. This is something that can be done – but it needs to be within a framework that keeps recovery as a task for the individual to come back to later on. The new, evolving, psychiatry is a humbler enterprise, something that will affect the future role of psychiatrists. Changes are taking place, forward steps are being taken and in places recovery models are being introduced. However, any visitor to an acute psychiatric ward will find that naïve psychiatry is still alive and well and doing brisk business.

Part I.
The Myth that Psychiatric Treatment Produces Recovery

Chapter 1
THE ORIGINS OF NAÏVE PSYCHIATRY

Myths are powerful ideas that exert their influence because we think they are true. They make up the fabric of our world. They are assumptions so natural that we assume they must be true. We may not like hearing our own beliefs described as "myths"; it may come over as rude and challenging, but that's what they are. We all need assumptions to be able to run our lives. They come to be seen as "myths" only when we start examining them closely. It is then that we can see their feet of clay.

I have been a psychiatrist all my adult life and so have worked within a particularly complicated framework of ideas. When things go well my experiences fit in with this framework and I am reassured that the ideas are sound, and based in reality. However, at other times I have my doubts. There is nothing to prove that these ideas are true, they are just one way of looking at things - they are in fact shared myths. My interest in recovery led me to question these assumptions. I had a growing awareness that medical treatment does not deliver the recovery that it promises. Worse than that, the medical approach to helping people with mental health problems can get in the way of the recovery that people find for themselves.

Recovery is part of the orthodox medical story, and always has been. The aim of doctors has been to diagnose the illness, deliver the correct treatment, and so bring about recovery; it is an "illness-treatment-recovery model". This is not a theory, or something that someone has claimed is true – it is just the way things are, part of the myth.

Psychiatrists find it difficult to grasp the newness of the ideas behind the "Recovery Movement" that is now gaining ground (R.Coleman 1999, G.Roberts & P.Wolfson 2004). They consider that they have always been working to get their patients to recover, yet now suddenly recovery is what everyone wants. It has become a popular, acceptable idea, something different from the standard medical approach. A variety of healthcareprofessionals - Psychologists, Community Psychiatric Nurses (CPNs) and Community Workers - now use a "recovery model" which includes drawing up "recovery programmes" for their patients or clients. The acceptance of this model signals the arrival of a softer, more acceptable psychiatry. This involves the individual playing a central part in planning their own treatment. Recovery in this sense is a key concept in the way that mental health services are being planned in the "New NHS" (Department of Health 2001). It is a concept that everyone is claiming as their own preserve and it marks a decisive step away from the way psychiatry has been organised in the past.

One of the main justifications for psychiatric intervention is that it will help the person to recover. This may seem very obvious, but it has not always been so. Historically there have been other things used to justify intervention. One is reminded of this when one finds that the British Journal of Psychiatry, (the official journal of British psychiatry), began life in 1853 as the Asylum Journal of Mental Science. It was in the asylums that psychiatry really got started, and for them containment of the mentally ill, and their segregation from society were the main goals. The prevention of harm being done to the public by dangerous mentally disturbed people was a big concern, and one justification for the asylum system. They were thus part of a Victorian approach to what is now called "risk management". This contrast with the second half of the twentieth century, when the idea of helping people to recover became central to the prestige and self-esteem of psychiatrists. The history of psychiatry during the last fifty years helps to explain how the myth that psychiatric treatment can bring about recovery became so firmly established. Now, at the beginning of a new century, the circle has turned again, and risk has once more become an over-riding concern for psychiatry. New priorities have been set for mental health services, based on the perceived high risk that the mentally ill pose to the general public.

There is a small but vital question that I have often been asked by people who are new to the mental health field. "Do the treatments used in psychiatry correct what is really wrong – are they curative, or do they simply reduce distress and alleviate symptoms? In other words, primarily

3

are they supportive?" The answers given go to the heart of any discussion about recovery. Ambitious therapists of all kinds want to claim that their interventions correct the underlying disorder, but the more cautious point out that there is no evidence of this.

The Sargant approach

Psychiatry has had a series of "great leaps forward". I encountered one when I was a medical student in the 1960's. At that time the development of physical methods of treatment was being proclaimed as a revolution. One of its evangelists was Dr William Sargant, Head of the Department of Psychological Medicine at St.Thomas's Hospital in London and the first psychiatrist I ever met. He was convinced that the new physical methods of treatments, - drugs, ECT and leucotomy were enabling him to treat and restore to a healthy life many who would previously have been untreatable. When he taught me he was approaching the end of his career and leucotomy was already discredited and out of fashion. However he remained positive and enthusiastic about other physical treatments. His book "Physical Methods of Treatment in Psychiatry" (Sargant & Slater 1964) which was translated into several languages and ran to many editions, presented the new approach in a practical way that enabled people to follow Sargent's example. It is like a cookbook - full of ideas about things to do to people to make them better. It is almost devoid of theory.

Sargant was an adventurous and heroic therapist who was prepared to try anything to get people into a remission. (Remission - a cessation of disturbing and distressing symptoms). He drew parallels between his treatments and the extreme physical and psychological pressures used in religious cults and "brain washing". The model was that, if disturbed and pathological patterns of thought could be sufficiently interrupted, then they would lose their hold on the person and normal patterns of thought would re-emerge. The methods used included combinations of drugs and ECT. He was a well-known figure in his day - always regarded as a bit of a maverick. He tended to go further than other psychiatrists. He took a pragmatic approach to what he did - claiming that it was justified because it worked. His main criticism of other approaches such as psychoanalysis was that they did not work.

Doctors in other parts of the country referred patients to him who had failed to respond to more conventional treatments. Many of these ended up on his in-patient unit at the Waterloo Hospital in London. Here patients could be put on a special narcosis regime. They were heavily sedated so that they slept 23 hours per day, were given high doses of medication and in some cases ECT as well. This could go on for up to six weeks. The aim was to get the patients into remission, to abate their symptoms. Dr Sargant claimed that his results were very good. The Unit had the atmosphere of a medical ward for very sick people. The nurses were very aware of the danger of patients becoming physically unwell on this regime and checked regularly to make sure they were not developing pneumonia or pressure sores. A similar approach, applied by a less careful psychiatrist, led to the Chelmsford Hospital scandal in Sydney, Australia in 1983. There was a major enquiry after 48 people died while being treated with a form of narcosis therapy.

Sargant's practice is now only of historical interest and many aspects of it would no longer be seen as acceptable. Even at the time he was regarded as a bit extreme. However he was a very convincing, persuasive psychiatrist, a charismatic figure who exerted a wide influence around the world through his writing and teaching. He did a lot to establish a certain style of psychiatry and was extremely positive about helping people, convinced that he could get many to recover who would otherwise be abandoned as hopeless cases. Many of his students went on to become psychiatrists, inspired more by his optimism than his methods. He was a bit of a showman - who genuinely believed in his own remedies. He was very keen on the drug Nardil - one of the monoamine oxidise inhibitor antidepressants. He believed it could cure a wide range of conditions. He told us that we should take it if we developed certain symptoms and said that he had prescribed it for his wife. I remember him extolling its virtues to one patient, telling him that he must have faith in it. The patient misheard this, and said yes, he did have faith; he went to church regularly. Dr.Sargant said no, that was not what he meant; he should have faith in Nardil. I remembered this episode much later when I read about another keen young psychiatrist, Dr Freud, who became so convinced about the benefits of a new drug, in his case cocaine, that he pressed his family and friends to take it.

Sargant has now passed into history, but his basic approach was enormously influential. He was trying, by whatever means he could, to get people into remission. This was done by the administration of drugs and/ or ECT. The medical profession at that time marvelled at their ability to treat people in this way. There was much talk of new treatments, revolutions and reference back to the dark days of the old asylums. It seemed that the long hoped-for cure for mental illness had at last arrived. This gave psychiatrists great confidence and fitted in well with the growing feeling that the old Victorian mental hospitals needed to close. It may be that the closure of the old institutions would not have had the support of the medical profession. without the optimistic model of psychiatry that Sargant did so much to support;

Just how much the advent of the physical treatments contributed to the run down in the numbers of patients in hospital is debatable. It seems that the rising tide of numbers in psychiatric hospitals turned in the early 1950's, a short time before the new treatments became widely available. However the drug treatments gave confidence to psychiatrists that in future they would be able to treat and discharge people who previously spent years in hospital. The hope, or myth, took root that medical treatments, if carried out with sufficient vigour would not only get people into remission, but also get them to recover. This is one source of the idea that recovery can be induced by medical treatment (particularly drugs); or that recovery is something that can be done to people, more or less regardless of their involvement.

This approach leaves out all reference to the person and their experience - the lack of psychology very much part of Sargant's style. He was very English, in a bluff, muscular, rugby-playing sort of way. Like most of his generation, he had survived the rigours of the Second World War and had also been through periods of life threatening illness, having spent long periods in a sanatorium being treated for tuberculosis. He set himself against psychoanalysis – as being meddlesome and unhelpful. His alternative was an all out assault on the symptoms of mental illness, so that people could then get on with their lives as best they could.

This was a "stiff upper lip" approach. It was very much in keeping with current thinking about how emotional difficulties should be resolved. We need to keep this in mind when earlier ideas about mental health are considered. A good way of coping with personal suffering and distress is not fixed by underlying biological mechanisms, it is strongly influenced by prevailing custom and expectation. Fifty years ago it was seen as normal to suppress bad feelings and deny distress. This formed a major component of the psychiatric approach taken to people who developed problems during World War II and was seen as having been much more effective than psychiatric practice during the first war. The emotional climate of the time can be glimpsed in films and novels of the period and can also be encountered by talking to people who went through World War II. Their ideas about how people should react to and deal with disturbing events are very different from those current today. The changes in what is regarded as good emotional health are very relevant to the evolution of ideas about recovery. They help explain why what was seen as getting people back to good mental health fifty years ago is no longer seen as adequate. It is only possible to understand what people want from recovery if one knows what they will accept as good mental health. This is not fixed but evolving.

The Sargant model of psychiatry has been very influential. It fitted in well with moves to destigmatise and normalise psychiatry. Claiming that mental illness is the same as any other illness was an important tactic in countering the gross neglect suffered by people with mental health problems. Modern treatment delivered in pleasant surroundings was needed. This was part of a liberal, humane movement that brought about a transformation of mental health services in Britain. I have been part of this, moving during my career from a run down Victorian asylum, to a new, purpose-built ward in a general hospital. This has led to a real rise in expectations of what can be done for people. The criticism of psychiatry, which has always gone on, and to which I am now contributing, is part of a continuing debate. It should not obscure the great progress that has taken place in the past thirty years.

There are many situations where the Sargant model still seems to work; which explains the survival of the underlying myth. A psychiatrist sees a lot of people presenting with an acute disturbance of mental function. They have intense, disturbing symptoms that make them unable to carry on. They may be depressed, hopeless and despairing to such an extent that they are determined to kill themselves. They may be deluded and responding to frightening auditory hallucinations, and they are convinced these are real.

They may have tried to kill someone because they thought that person was going to attack them. In each case, the person's mental state has become seriously disturbed - it is an urgent necessity that it should return to normal. These are the sorts of situations where treatment can be imposed against someone's will allowable - under the Mental Health Act. These are the hard cases that any account of the subject needs to cover.

In these acute situations psychiatric treatments have much to offer. The situations are fraught and sometimes dangerous; they encompass extremes of human experience and behaviour rarely encountered in every-day life. When faced with such cases it is important to have clear plans and the authority to make sure they are carried out. These are times when the highest priority is to produce a change in the mental state of the person. Treatment in such situations remains effective and rewarding to carry out. It is generally possible to bring people into a remission. If the aim of the acute intervention is to relieve the severe symptoms that led to the crisis, then that target can nearly always be reached.

Achieving results in these types of crises may be seen as a complete vindication of orthodox psychiatry. For example, people who suffer from psychotic episodes, with symptoms such as delusions and hallucinations, may lose their symptoms completely following treatment with antipsychotic medication. It is because this is seen as such a routine result that recovery is not seen as a big problem by many psychiatrists. The acute, short-term treatment of people like this has been the key training experience for most workers in psychiatry. It has been the paradigm of what it is to help someone with acute severe mental health problems, the "medical model" at its best. However, since key elements in emergencies are: the imposition of treatment; physical control and restraint; and use of the law, it could equally well be called the judicial or legal model.

Case study Kate

Kate was a young woman bringing up her daughter on her own. Her problems got steadily worse over many months. She developed the idea that she and her daughter were being attacked by the IRA who had been paid by her ex-partner to kill her. She began to barricade her flat, and refuse to let her daughter go out. She reported hearing the terrorists making crude comments about her outside her window. There was great concern because she would not go out to buy food, and lack of sleep was making her worse. Her mother and a social worker had been able to talk to her through the letterbox, but then one morning there was no answer from her. A warrant was obtained from a magistrate, and the front door broken down by the police. We found her and her daughter cowering in a bedroom, terrified by the sound of the assault on her flat. She was admitted to hospital against her wishes, and remained angry and distressed about what had happened. She was convinced that the hospital was in league with her would-be assassins. She had to be forced to have injections of antipsychotic medication, and believed that she was going to be killed. I had to go on treating her in the face of her anger and hostility. Then after about six weeks she began to improve. In time she lost all her symptoms. She was able to agree that she had been deluded. She agreed to continue taking antipsychotic medication after she went home. She became warm and friendly towards the ward staff - to whom she had previously been so hostile.

This case is an example of success achieved by conventional - and not particularly sophisticated - psychiatric treatment. It looks on the face of it like an open and shut case. The outcome seems to justify the heavy handed methods that had to be used. Such cases affirm doctors in the correctness of their actions. They confirm the need at times to ignore what someone is saying, and decide for them what is best. At the time I and the others involved were confident that Kate had made a good recovery. Her case stood out as having a good outcome, and is the sort of example that strengthens belief in the medical model. However there were later developments in this case, to which I will return.

This case may be seen as a vindication of the Sargant model. In the psychiatric literature it tends to be offered as just that. Studies of treatment generally involve measuring symptoms on a large series of rating scales before and then shortly after a short-term intervention. This is what stands for recovery in psychiatry. The great majority of treatment studies into schizophrenia – to take one example - involve follow-up of no more than a few months. If Kate had been assessed using symptom rating scales she would have been judged to have fully recovered. For many working in psychiatry the experience of getting very disturbed people into remission is the core of the discipline. It is seen as self-evidently justified and worthwhile.

In Sargant's day he was sent 'cases' from all over the country. They would receive intensive treatment, hopefully go into symptomatic remission, and then return home.   When I first worked in psychiatric hospitals the situation was similar. We would treat people in hospital, with little contact with the outside world, and they would settle down. We prided ourselves on getting people better. They then went home after which the only contact would be brief, rather stilted interviews in the outpatient clinic. It was easy to become complacent. It was a system that seemed to work well. It conformed well to the "illness-treatment-recovery" model. Kate's case is an example of this.

Confessions of a Naïve Psychiatrist

The picture began to change for me when I started to get to know my patients better, and to remain in touch with them for long periods after they had gone home. I was also influenced by talking to ex-patients who took on the role of mediating between the patients and the professionals. I was now responsible for a catchment area. This meant that anyone from that area who developed serious mental illness became my responsibility. I had to treat them however I thought best, using the resources that were available. These included a ward in a psychiatric unit, a number of nursing staff and latterly a community mental health centre. I looked after the same patch for twenty years - so I got to know the patients from that area very well. I had never been convinced that people with psychiatric illness followed the clear patterns described in the textbooks of psychiatry. However the longer I was in touch with the same population, the less easy it was to fit each person with a useful diagnosis. The other casualty of this greater familiarity with people's lives was the "illness-treatment-recovery" model. It was still possible to see symptomatic improvement during spells of treatment in hospital - but when I met people later I would question whether they had "really" recovered.

It began to be obvious to me that many of those who were our priority patients – those with serious mental illness - did not lose their symptoms following treatment. They needed long-term medication, yet appeared stuck, held back by their illness. They would often strive to shake off psychiatry, for instance by seeking to break off contact or stop medication as soon as they could. We would then have to make great efforts to draw them back into the world of psychiatry. The struggle that people put up to break away from us seemed to me an impressive show of spirit - from people who otherwise were having difficulty finding any way of asserting themselves. If we succeeded we would manage to get them "re-engaged with services", and as likely as not back on medication. But at what cost? And for what benefit?

Case study Michael

Michael was an ex-paratrooper who was living with his partner when I first met him. Before that he had spent most of the preceding ten years in and out of psychiatric hospitals. He had a diagnosis of paranoid schizophrenia. He did not like this diagnosis, and often brought up the subject when he was angry or disturbed. He hated the fact that he had been given that diagnosis. He got on well with his partner, but continued to have complicated delusions. He believed that he had become a Russian spy and that because of this he was being bombarded with radiation by the Americans. He also thought the country was being taken over by communists and that he was going to have to play a leading part. His ideas were certainly bizarre, and when I first met him I found it difficult to know how to respond to his statements. He had been put on large doses of antipsychotic medication in hospital, and he continued to ask for and accept the injections. His condition varied in severity. At times he would become agitated and excited. He would then shout at people he thought were persecuting him, and because of his threatening manner he would be admitted to hospital. At other times he could be relaxed and pleasant, and enjoy wide ranging discussions about the state of the country. Michael's attitude to his condition varied over the years that I knew him. At times he wanted to take medication, sometimes he refused it, often he asked for it to be changed. Sometimes he complained about side effects from the medication, and at one time he went to a solicitor to see if he could sue me for giving him harmful drugs. Over many years Michael suffered, and did not get much better or much worse. I was never convinced that his medication did him much good, and he certainly suffered from terrible side-effects, including disfiguring abnormal movements and sexual dysfunction. He survived and carried on with his life, but it was not what my medical training led me to regard as recovery. There was no real remission of symptoms. Yet over the years I came to admire Michael, and to appreciate the quality of his ability to survive. From being someone with no life at all, stuck in a hospital, he had fashioned a life for himself. In struggling for what he wanted he often appeared wilfully contrary. He would stick to what he wanted to do and would not do the recommended thing. It was only after long acquaintance that I realised that it was not the symptoms of schizophrenia that were ruining his life but his poverty, unemployment, bad housing and social ostracisation. He was frequently humiliated in the streets, with youths shouting at him and threatening him. His recovery, the life that he was able to fashion for himself, was achieved in spite of my efforts to treat him. I began to realise that to work with him I would have to modify my approach.

Kate's case did not end with the one episode described above. I met her again several years later, when she was having another psychotic episode. She was again frightened and paranoid. This time her daughter was old enough to look after herself, and she was determined to avoid hospital treatment. She had vivid memories of the police breaking into her flat. She also remembered the medication that she had been forced to take. I reminded her how well she had responded to treatment, but she would not accept that at all. . She said that when I had been treating her before she had been terrified that her daughter would be taken away, and so would have agreed to anything to get out of hospital. She said that the medication had upset her periods and made her put on weight, so that she stopped it as soon as she got home, but went on saying that she was taking it. This was all quite a shock for me. It changed the impression I had had, and presented my own role in what had happened in a very different light. Kate had appeared to make such a good straight-forward recovery following medical treatment, but now I was not so sure. It was the ability to produce recovery that justified the compulsory treatment of Kate. The treatment certainly achieved the short term goals - which included ensuring the safety of her and her daughter, but at what cost to her long-term recovery?

By the time I was working in the NHS of the 1980's and 90's, the drug treatments were no longer new, and were being given to a population that generally did not like them. In many cases the remission of symptoms, (the justification for this approach), was only partly achieved. Many of those on long-term antipsychotic medication still had lives dominated by their psychotic symptoms, and still suffered from periodic worsening of their condition, requiring re-admission to hospital. Those with recurrent mood disturbances remained on antidepressants and also on mood stabilising drugs This may only to be expected, and those in favour of drug treatment argue that by remaining on the drugs their problems are at least less intense. However it goes further than this. Many who have long term mental health problems live lives dominated by treatment. Having therapy becomes a way of life. Therapy groups can certainly be supportive and helpful but they remain therapy groups and those attending are still dependent on the mental health care system.

The "illness-treatment-recovery" model has been the prevailing one in hospitals and clinics. It holds out the idea that a successful outcome from treatment is that it will get you into remission. You will then be able to get on with your life. However, I found that, according to this model, most of the people treated by me were failures. They did not attain this goal. This is a depressing finding. Was I doing it wrong? Had I somehow failed to learn how to treat people?

Looking for 'real' recovery

My interest in recovery grew. Was it something that might be achieved if I treated people differently? There is often publicity about some psychiatrist who gives patients a striking or "heroic" treatment, and claims wonderful results. All kinds of odd treatments have had their day. These are often things that are not really new - but are done with great conviction and given a fancy name. They may involve a drug that is available for any doctor to use, but which, somehow, in the hands of the guru, achieves marvellous results. The literature tends to give the impression that if only the doctors and nurses and psychologists were clever enough then the patients would get better. Cases described all seem to do incredibly well. It is all a matter of having enough staff with the right training. There is a systematic exaggeration of the benefits of treatment. If people do not get better it is put down to lack of "resources".

I began to think back over the hundreds of people who I had treated to remember some who had "really" recovered. I formed the idea that if I could identify a group of people who had made a complete recovery, studying them and learning from them would help answer my question. Around that time I had an encounter which cast more doubt on the whole question. While trying to remember patients who might be examples complete recovery I had vivid memories of a man I had treated about ten years before.

Case study: Anthony

Anthony was an estate agent who occupied a prominent position in the local business community and had experienced a severe manic episode. He had become completely obsessed with a project he was pursuing and ended up being admitted to hospital under Section 2 of the Mental Health Act. He had responded quickly and well to medication. He was a pleasant, likeable man who within a few days of admission to hospital regained insight into what had been happening to him. He was then able to cooperate with treatment. Soon he was having periods of leave at home, and within a few weeks he was discharged. He came to see me in the outpatient clinic, where he appeared smart, business-like, and thoroughly back to normal. We talked about the pressures he was under from his hectic life-style, and he talked about the need to make changes.

Anthony was referred back to see me again; at about the time I was trying to think of people who had done particularly well. In fact thinking about him I had felt he would not have been a very instructive case to review, as his psychiatric problem had been so simple and straight forward.

When I saw him again I had to revise this assessment. He was now suffering from depression, with worryingly definite thoughts of suicide. He said that since his episode ten years before his life had gone down hill. His marriage had broken up and he had lost his original job - both due to his behaviour during his manic episode. He suffered a lot from guilt about the break up of his family and the effect on his children. He also had bad memories of his psychosis. He remembered feelings of great power and great responsibility. He could also picture many of the embarrassing things he had done. He had tried a number of different jobs, but they were never at the same level as his old job. At times when he was depressed he knew his concentration was not so good - and he was not so sharp.

This story was not exceptional. It confirms what has been shown by a number of long-term follow-up studies. People who suffer major mood disorders tend to have continuing problems and do not lose their disorder once they have been put on the right medication. In other words controlling the symptoms does not lead to recovery from the disorder. It underlined my growing awareness that the naive optimism of Sargant was bound to lead to disappointment. I realised that when I first treated Anthony I had let him down. I went along too quickly with his naive optimism, his belief that everything would be all right. I thought I had done a good job getting him through the acute episode. In fact the worst part was after he left us - something for which I did nothing to prepare him.

There is a powerful element of denial in the hope that things will miraculously return to how they were. It is unfair to give treatment saying that it will bring about recovery - yet knowing it will not; saying that the treatment is enough to make an average person better - so if it doesn't work for you, then it must be your fault. Giving directions, yet knowing that nobody reaches the destination.

There was a vital part of Sargant's teaching that I have not mentioned. He set great store by his patients being of "good, sound personality". In his day there was less concern about using critical, prejudicial language, and what he wrote was this:

"Simple physical-treatment methods will help most of the anxiety states, depressions, and schizophrenic illnesses in patients of good previous personality... Nor can we make the patient of previously chronically inadequate personality into someone with an adequate one. ...All we can really seem to do at the present time in psychiatry is to restore the status quo." (Sargant 1966)

Sargant was not responsible for a catchment area and was able to choose those he would take on for treatment. Before embarking on his heroic treatments he had to be satisfied that the person had previously had a strong and healthy personality. This is not a sophisticated sort of assessment, just checking that the person was free of major problems before they developed their current symptoms. To qualify as a good case for treatment someone would have to have a reasonable employment record, have had at least some good relationships, been free of persistent neurotic symptoms, and not be reliant on drugs or alcohol. It is in people who met these criteria that he achieved good results. He was good at selecting those who would show a good response. The people he treated were thus very different from those who have confronted the generations of "catchment-area psychiatrists", such as me, who were to follow him. We have had to treat whoever was referred for treatment. This has always included a large percentage of people who would probably have been rejected by Sargant as having "inadequate personalities". Freed of prejudicial language this means those who have complex and continuing problems, i.e. the target population for NHS psychiatry.

On a positive note it remains true that acute, intensive medical intervention can still achieve the good results that Sargant described. This achieved remission of symptoms in the case of Kate. If someone develops acute, intrusive psychotic symptoms they may place themselves and others at risk. The Mental Health Act exists to allow for the treatment of people in this state. It is a person's right to have such treatment provided, in as humane a setting as possible. There is now a wider range of options than in Sargant's day - with the introduction of home treatment teams. The aim of acute intervention is still to produce remission of symptoms. This can usually be achieved with the help of medication, and intensive support.

My conclusion from the case of Kate, and many others, is that successful medical treatment of acute episodes can lead to remission, but not recovery. It is really a kind of first aid. This goes back to the simple, vital issue of whether the treatments really are curative, in the sense of making the underlying problem better, or supportive in the sense of just calming the person and suppressing the high level of distress that is making them unable to function. If acute interventions are seen as first aid; necessary but essentially supportive operations; it will be clear that once they are finished, the process of recovery will need to continue for a long time. Far from being achieved by vigorous medical treatment, recovery may be interrupted and delayed by it. The stress of treatment may be part of what someone has to recover from. These are paradoxes that I wish to explore.

The Medical Idea of Recovery

My difficulty with recovery goes back to my medical training. The concept that has been applied in psychiatry is borrowed from medicine. It holds out the idea that people will simply "get back to normal", and then be just as they were before. This is a child's view of what happens when you become unwell. Children are familiar with minor conditions such as cuts and bruises, coughs and colds. They also come across more serious conditions such as broken bones and appendicitis. For these conditions there is consultation with a doctor, who prescribes some treatment. For a broken bone there is immobilisation with plaster, and for appendicitis there is a simple operation to remove the diseased appendix. For these conditions, the healing process occurs because of mechanisms at work in the body. Treatment is supportive, aiming to provide good conditions for the body's natural processes to be able to function, and to stop anything getting in the way of natural healing. It is not really fair to credit the treatment with the fact that your cut finger has healed up. What happens in the body is a wonder of nature, a mystery, not something brought about by a doctor.

The impression received as a child is that recovery involves getting back to normal. In this the role of the patient is essentially passive. As long as the patient does not actively interfere with recovery, then it will just happen. Recovery from mental illness is often presented as analogous to this; a simple going back to how you were before – or as Sargant put it, restoration of the status quo. It should result in you being able to feel the same, and capable of doing the same things as before.

There are several odd things about this notion of recovery: It is too good to be true. It is complete and leaves no problems behind.

It may be argued that surely people are not so naïve; surely they would not expect this after mental illness. After all, it is difficult enough to find an example of a physical illness from which recovery is so complete. I believe this concept of recovery is part of the oversimplified medical model that forms part of the culture of psychiatry, the "illness-treatment-recovery model".

This approach is what I call "naïve psychiatry". It is not a theory put forward by anyone but I am sure that it has been an assumption underlying much recent psychiatry. It focuses on short term improvements in symptoms as a main target for intervention. Although its origins are over fifty years old, and it reflects an outdated concept of what it is to recover from mental illness, it is still very much in evidence. There is a continuing crisis in acute psychiatry with many units having over 100% occupancy rates, and high rates of compulsory admission. Brief reductions in symptoms and just enough improvement in function to enable a person to be discharged become the best that can be hoped for. Yet putting people through this system is not getting them to recover, but often damaging and alienating them.

Growing doubts.

I am chronicling my own struggles towards understanding. I confess to having practised "Naïve Psychiatry" for many years. In the early 1990's a sea change was occurring in the mental health field in the U.K. The old psychiatric institutions were closing with the patients and staff moving on to new places. But they were the same people – in new places, and it was not easy to shake off the culture of the old system. I am an example of that process. I started in psychiatry working in a Victorian County Asylum. It was struggling to shake off its old custodial associations – but they were all around us. There were dormitories where patients slept - huge rooms, rows of beds with barely space to stand up between them. There was a large mansion in the grounds where the head psychiatrist lived, his garden tended by the long stay patients. Yet there was good work going on. The enormity of the task made the work a challenge and a cause to which many people dedicated their lives. Inside the old repressive institution there were some inspiring areas and projects which brought hope; but there was also great suffering for those trapped within the system.

The more I got to know about the lives of people affected by mental illness, the more uncertain I became. It wasn't just that "getting people to recover" was proving to be very difficult, though it was. I was becoming aware that the quality of life of some people, who we thought were doing well, was really very poor.

I remained aware of the limitations that Sargant and his followers had placed on what they could achieve. They had selected out certain conditions that they thought would respond to vigorous physical treatment, and excluded everyone else. There was a very dark side to this. I remember the consternation on Sargant's unit if the "wrong sort of patients" turned up. People suffering from severe and continuing problems were immediately assessed as not cases for treatment. They sometimes turned up in the casualty department, seeking help. As a new student I had to accompany such a person, sent in an ambulance to one of the large mental hospitals in a remote outlying area.

I came across the same practice of selecting who should be treated when I was training in the 1970's. We ran a very disciplined, controlled service. We treated people with syndromes for which there were well established treatments. We expected our patients to be reasonable and cooperative. Any challenging or difficult behaviour would quickly lead to a diagnosis of personality disorder, and if problems continued the person would be discharged.

The naïve psychiatry model was designed to treat those who did not have complex and difficult problems. They were people who had functioned well, but had become temporarily overwhelmed by psychological symptoms. They were the group for whom recovery as a return to how you were before was particularly appropriate. Indeed, they were selected for this very reason. One place where this approach still gets a lot of support is in private hospitals, where selection processes continue to operate.

I applied the same medical treatments to patients presenting within my catchment area, but the results did not match those described in the textbooks. My patients may have been accepting treatment and shown some improvement in symptoms, - but at what cost? Often they were badly affected by the side effects of medication, and leading lives of physical, emotional and spiritual impoverishment. In those days one of the great innovations was the introduction of long-acting injectable anti-psychotic medication. Patients could be discharged from hospital and then kept well by having regular injections – often for many years. It was a tremendous breakthrough. However when this regime had been in operation for many years the seriousness of the side-effects of the drugs began to be widely recognised. They included impotence, loss of feelings, abnormal movements and loss of drive. The side-effects had been known to doctors from the start, but it was many years before it was realised just how much suffering they caused. Up to that point the professional view was that the side effects were a 'price worth paying', since the drugs were shown to prevent relapses. Only when the people taking the drugs began to speak out was it realised that not all of them were prepared to pay such a high price. This raised for me the question of whether the lives some people had on these drugs really constituted recovery. Eliminating symptoms and recovering might be two very different things.

At the same time that I was beginning to doubt the quality of the recovery provided by my treatments, I was coming to admire some other patients, who on the face of it were resisting all attempts to get them to recover. They were leading quite desperate and dangerous lives, apparently prepared to risk all in order to maintain their fragile independence. These were people who seemed wilfully to resist all efforts to get them to comply with treatment. They would say that they did not like the side effects, or that they were against drugs on principle. Such views were uncommon in the days when most treatment took place in hospital, but became much more common once people were leading more independent lives.

Nietzsche's paradox

These thoughts grew as time went on. They were uncomfortable for someone earning his living from practising psychiatry. Was I becoming a renegade psychiatrist – one who was abandoning his principles – a turncoat? Or was I just showing the all too familiar signs of burnout?

There is a paradox which has sustained me through my time of loss of faith - I call it "Nietzsche's Paradox", after the great destroyer of idols. I had come to doubt the claims made for many of the specific treatments used in psychiatry. The claims made by the professors of psychopharmacology and the drug companies for their products were never fulfilled in practice. The new clever therapies never seemed to produce the transformations that they promised. And as time went on I could see less and less value in the elaborate systems of diagnosis and classification that are so central to psychiatry. Yet discarding those articles of faith did not leave me in a state of despair and nihilism. On the contrary I felt liberated. I was no longer relying on things in which I did not believe, but I became more aware of the power and effectiveness of the non-specific factors which help people to recover. The fact that theories are unhelpful and the treatments don't live up to expectations does not leave people empty handed. In fact, I found it easier to help people in distress once I had acknowledged my doubts.

Nietzsche's Paradox is about the liberating and enlightening effect of giving up precisely those ideas that you used to think were necessary to make sense of the field. You don't know anything, until you know that you don't know anything.

There was a recent small furore when a senior executive in a drug company admitted that most of the high profile drugs will not work at all for a sizeable proportion of those who are given them. This has always been obvious to doctors, but has rarely been said in public. It has not affected the enthusiasm of doctors for prescribing drugs. If only 50% derive benefit from the drugs, why are 100% are still being encouraged to take them? The 50% who do not benefit may be positively disadvantaged by the unwanted effects of the drug. Efforts to raise the amount that patients actually take of the prescribed drugs fail to address well-founded patient scepticism.

The oversimplified concept of recovery that is borrowed from medicine turns out to be unattainable. Paradoxically it turns out that being over optimistic has a depressing effect; it makes it appear that most people have a poor outcome. This is one factor contributing to the pessimistic attitudes that one finds in mental health services. The conclusion is that the recovery promised by psychiatric treatment is too often a myth (Whitwell.1999), an over optimistic idea based on a false analogy between mental illness and simple physical illness.

Chapter 2
ASKING PSYCHIATRISTS AND THEIR PATIENTS ABOUT RECOVERY

I began my study of recovery with the idea that the kind of recovery that medical treatments promised was genuine enough, even if not very common. I therefore thought that there would be some amongst the patients treated by me and my colleagues who would have made good, complete recoveries. They might be exceptions to the rule, but it would be all the more interesting to find them and talk to them, in order to understand the processes involved. I was working in a busy psychiatric unit serving a population of 250,000, so I thought there should be plenty of subjects. I explained to the psychiatrists working in the unit that I wanted them to select people who in their judgement had recovered from their psychiatric illness following treatment. There were questions about what I meant by "recovery". I said that it is not a technical term, and that they could decide whom they thought it would apply to. It was agreed that it was a term that was in use, and that some people were said to have recovered.

It was hoped that interviews with people who had recovered would provide qualitative data about the experience of recovery; what it was like to have recovered and how people could tell that they had reached that point. It was also hoped to elicit views about factors that had contributed to recovery. This would not distinguish between people's theories about what had affected them, and what actually had affected them. It was intended to be an exploratory, preliminary study.

I did not conduct the interviews. As an established local psychiatrist I would not have been impartial enough to be asking people about their experiences. Bree Macdonald, a young woman with a degree in psychology who had not at that time worked in the mental health field, assisted me.

A pilot study was done in order to check that the interview was covering the right areas and catching the right information. I had previously been in contact with a support group for users of mental health services. I asked them for volunteers for the pilot study, saying that I wanted people who considered that they had recovered from psychiatric illness.

The interviews with ten subjects went well. Information about the experience of recovery seemed to be readily available. However the results at first seemed disappointing and cast doubt on the future of the project. Although the subjects had volunteered as people who had recovered and were prepared to talk about it, their accounts did not really fit with what we expected. They all reported major continuing problems in their lives due to their psychiatric illness. These included persisting symptoms, reduced tolerance of stress, restricted lifestyles, unemployment, stigma and poverty. They made remarks such as –

"Yes, but I will never be the same person again".

"I have made a good recovery, but I wouldn't say I have recovered. As to making a full recovery, I don't know if you ever do".

"I do consider that I have recovered, but I think it will take a bit longer to forget".

The volunteers tended to see themselves as survivors, and from their accounts it was clear why they preferred that term. None of them could see themselves as having definitely recovered. Also, they saw their passage through the mental health services as contributing almost as much to their difficulties as the mental illness itself. They were thus survivors of treatment as well as illness.

The next stage was to interview subjects selected by their psychiatrist. At first the psychiatrists had said that they did not think there would be any difficulty in identifying subjects. In practice it turned out to be difficult. Over a nine-month period only thirteen could be identified. This was too small a group to enable us to come to firm conclusions. However, the failure to find more people who had "recovered from psychiatric illness" was itself of interest. What the subjects said was similar to the views of the pilot study.

This was itself interesting - counteracting as it does the common claim that user groups are self-selected and biased, and thus unrepresentative of psychiatric patients in general. This issue is important because user groups are now becoming involved in advising health authorities about how to develop mental health services. The patients selected by the psychiatrists would have been expected to be model patients, chosen for their compliance and acceptance of the medical system. However they seemed similar to the self-selected members of the user group. Almost all the subjects wanted to take issue with the concept of recovery. They wanted to say that they had "not really recovered". They were strongly aware of not being the same as they had been. They were more careful, less confident, and more aware of danger.

A few reported on positive changes. They said that they were now more genuine, more their real self, more sensitive to other people. However, the feeling of "not being the same", was felt to be inconsistent with the concept of recovery.

The subjects were very conscious of their impaired life position following their psychiatric illness. They described unemployment, divorce, housing problems, lack of money and social isolation. They also described continuing psychological sequelae to their illness including recurrent unpleasant memories, loss of self-confidence and reduced tolerance of stress.

These subjects were selected as likely to report a good outcome to their psychiatric problems. They had not been coached on the subject of recovery - yet tended to agree that this was the desired outcome, but something that they had not attained. Their psychiatrists thought they were cases of this elusive thing "recovery", but they did not agree. It appeared the subjects were applying the old Medical Model criterion of success to themselves - and so failing themselves.

This brings back the idea of recovery as a myth. It is dangled in front of people as the hoped-for outcome of medical treatment, but unfortunately very few get there. It is a myth that has a wide currency in the mental health services. It is the rule of thumb criterion against which success or failure of treatment is judged. This must have a demoralising effect on staff. It means that the most of the people being treated will be regarded as having an unsatisfactory outcome. It must have the same effect on the person being treated. If those selected as having the best outcome think they have not done very well, what about the others?

This medical concept of recovery is left over from the old-fashioned oversimplified medical model of fifty years ago. Psychiatry has moved forwards in some ways but it has an inheritance of old fashioned medical concepts that persist. This is not a harmless academic problem. There have been decades of clever debate about the different models available for understanding mental health problems - but little progress. This in itself should make us suspicious that there is something fishy about these so-called philosophical problems. It is time to develop a concept of recovery that accords with people's real experience.

Chapter 3
THE CHALLENGE TO THE MEDICAL MODEL

Early in my study of recovery I spoke to a woman who had been through years of psychiatric treatment and later trained as a researcher in the field. On the basis of her writings she had become well respected and had been advising government agencies about mental health policy. I asked her how our services could do more help people to recover. Her view was unequivocal. In order to recover, people have to get away from psychiatry and psychiatrists. This rather cut the ground from under a psychiatrist who thought he could help people to recover. This opinion was not unusual. Since that time I have found that many of the people who have a special interest in mental health matters are hostile to psychiatry and its world-view. For example Alison Reeves writing a chapter in a book called "Early Intervention in Psychosis" (2000) edited by Birchwood et al wrote

"Between the Survivor movement and psychiatry lies a void of understanding about what recovery is. For the service users, mental illness is the mind's way of coping with extreme trauma and conflict, emotional abandonment and social isolation. Recovery is about being loved and accepted, finding your true self and your gifts and talents. It is about human transformation in the deepest sense.

For psychiatry, recovery is about obliterating or containing a brain disease at whatever cost to the individual. Recovery here means that the symptoms are under control and the person is compliant with treatment. While being on depot medication might be better for your prognosis in psychiatric terms (and less work for the professionals), it is not necessarily better for your recovery prospects."

Reeves goes on at length about her total opposition to the medical way of treating people. What is significant is that she is not a lone outsider but a member of an innovative project who was invited to contribute to a leading publication.

The antimedical challenge to orthodox psychiatry is serious and much more than just a clash of theories. It arises from deeply held convictions shared by a significant section of the population. Psychiatrists tend to see it as a marginal and insignificant issue, but that underestimates it. One of the factors that prevent such ideas from having a wider appeal is that they are presented as being naïve and incompatible with the harsh reality of working in the field. They have tended to be favoured by alternative therapists - people seen as remote from the "coal face" of acute psychiatry. This is no longer true, and many of those who work in mental health are uncomfortable with the "Medical Model". The criticisms are now more widespread, and find expression in many government statements on mental health. An unreformed medical model now seems old fashioned; yet it plays a large part in shaping the concept of recovery that is widely accepted.

Official government policy is confusing on the subject of the Medical Model. On the one hand there are ever growing lists of directives to mental health services to respect the rights, wishes and dignity of users of services, but at the same time there are moves to widen the use of compulsory treatment. This confusion reflects the conflicting pressures existing in society.

The anti-psychiatry of the 1960's and 70's was a challenge to orthodox thinking, but it came from within the same framework of ideas as was being attacked. The prevailing ideas and theories of medical orthodoxy were being challenged by alternative ideas and theories. Anti-psychiatry writers such as Laing and Foudraine recognised many of the things which are wrong with psychiatry and which still concern those who now oppose it. They began certain themes, which are now finally finding constructive expression. The U.K. government's National Service Framework published in 1999, the blueprint for how services should develop in the next ten years, contains many aspects that first found expression in the writings of anti-psychiatrists. However most anti-psychiatry writers went on to develop their own theories and principles, just as much open to distortion and abuse as the original targets of their critique. The challenge today does not come from ambitious, off-beat professionals seeking attention for their own ideas, but from people who have been through the system and can now speak up for themselves. Increasing numbers of people who have received psychiatric treatment are being employed within services to make use of their first hand experience. This challenge to the medical view is altogether more sustained and credible than anything seen in the past.

Opponents of psychiatry focus on the features of the Medical Model (MM). This term tends to make psychiatrists irritated and feel misunderstood. They say that no such simple model is followed by all psychiatrists. They say that the model that is generally followed should be called an eclectic or a bio-psycho-social model. Psychiatrists dislike being depicted as narrow-minded people who focus exclusively on biological factors.

The term Medical Model is used as shorthand for the salient aspects of what psychiatrists do - and it is not meant to describe a particular theoretical stance. What I have called "Naïve Psychiatry" – which sees remission of symptoms as equivalent to recovery - is very much the type of psychiatry widespread in the NHS today. This is what most people mean by the Medical Model. It is the psychiatry enshrined in the Mental Health Act, and enforced by the full might of the law. Psychiatrists are involved in the Medical Model, but it is so much more than any particular medical approach. It involves:

- Diagnosis: identifying the illnesses that people are suffering from
- Drugs as a mainstay of treatment
- Electro convulsive therapy
- Compulsion to make people go into hospital and accept treatment

As a professional one can become accustomed to each of these, and learn to overlook the fact that they continue to give rise to detailed and searching criticism.

Diagnosis of mental illness

There are difficulties in diagnosing illness which occur in many branches of medicine, but they are particularly acute in psychiatry. It is easy for a diagnosis to be misinterpreted. The names of psychiatric illnesses tend to have non-specialist meanings. Schizophrenia can mean so many different things that to tell someone that that is their diagnosis is at best uninformative, and at worst frightening and misleading. It is similar to telling someone that they are suffering from cancer, the message may do more harm than good. The shock of the diagnosis means that detailed explanation is needed straight away.

There is an argument that the diagnostic terms used in psychiatry are not purely objective clinical descriptions, but include critical, pejorative overtones. Thus "paranoid schizophrenia" and "personality disorder" are not labels that anyone would want to have applied to themselves.

But there is a more radical argument against psychiatric diagnosis: that the illnesses being named are not real. They are simply ways of categorising people - and not helpful. People are given the same diagnosis because they have similar symptoms, but they may not have much else in common. There will be far more things distinguishing them from each other. The whole point of medical or surgical diagnosis is that it indicates what is wrong with the person. A surgeon cannot get started without a diagnosis: the diagnosis is vital if treatment is to get at the cause of the trouble. In psychiatry, by contrast, the diagnosis does not indicate an underlying disturbance or lesion that can be got at and treated, because after 100 years of research no underlying pathology has been discovered. There are no physical ways of identifying psychiatric conditions. The justification of psychiatric diagnosis remains pragmatic – i.e. that it helps decide what treatment will be helpful for people with a certain diagnosis. "Not so" say the opponents, treatment needs to be based on individual needs and problems. As long as people are classified into the large groups called illnesses, psychiatrists are unable to focus on them as individuals.

There is also the Laingian argument. This maintains that, in diagnosing someone, you are deliberately adopting a particularly detached and distant attitude towards them. This can then easily lead to a cold and clinical type of relationship – which rather than being helpful is damaging.

The question of whether diagnosis in psychiatry is useful has been going on for a long time. The arguments have been summarised by Philip Thomas in "The Dialectics of Schizophrenia" (1997). There are strong things to say on each side. Many psychiatrists have some sympathy for the criticism of diagnosis, and place low importance on it when making treatment decisions. If the importance of the diagnostic system depends on its usefulness, the conclusion might be that it is not very important because it is not very useful. An alternative approach is to base decisions on the actual symptoms and problems that people have. Once one stops trying to make sense of "schizophrenia" and instead focuses on hallucinations, or particular kinds of hallucination, then progress can be made. Richard Bentall in " Explained" (2003) has summarised a lot of research into individual features of psychosis and how they can be helped.

Bentall is able to do this because he is a psychologist. For a psychiatrist the fact remains that having a diagnosis is still central to medical ways of understanding people with mental health problems. If I, as a psychiatrist, were to say to a court or a tribunal that after assessing someone's condition I was not making a diagnosis, the inference would be that there was nothing wrong with the person. If I said that they had serious problems, but I did not choose to make a diagnosis, it would call into question whether I was acting as a psychiatrist at all.

Thus making diagnoses is an essential part of psychiatry, and those who find the whole business questionable will have radical difficulty accepting any psychiatric view. The centrality of diagnosis to psychiatry explains why psychiatrists have not dealt with this issue. It is a bit like asking the church to consider the claims of atheism. There is a whole world of psychiatric literature, and much of it only makes sense on the assumption that there are separate mental illnesses. If that particular way of classifying people was discarded then much of the literature would become pointless. The difficulty of dispensing with diagnosis was shown in early work such as that done by R.D.Laing on the subject of schizophrenia. He wanted to advance theories about schizophrenia, but at the same time said that making this diagnosis was unhelpful, and damaging. The trouble was that since he did not make the diagnoses properly in the first place, there was no way that he could prove that he was talking about people who orthodox psychiatrists would regard as having schizophrenia. He could not enter the discourse on schizophrenia without diagnosing people as having that condition.

A diagnosis sums someone up in a single word or phrase. This is almost always misleading; for instance many people who have a diagnosis of schizophrenia suffer from low mood and are at risk of suicide. These may be more important when one is thinking of offering help than the consideration of more well known psychotic symptoms.

The failure of the diagnostic groupings to yield useful results after all these years does suggest that in future different strategies will be needed. These could focus on more clear-cut symptoms or problems. This however is some way off.

Drugs as a mainstay of treatment

Opponents of psychiatry have no difficulty pointing out all the drawbacks of drug treatment. These include:

- Unpleasant side effects
- Dependence on drugs not being a way forward
- Doubts about effectiveness

There is a long history of doctors minimising the problems that drugs cause, right up to the point where the drug has to be withdrawn. Drugs used to treat mental illness are certainly dangerous. In the past the decision about the balance of risks making it a good idea for someone to take a drug was taken by the doctor with limited consultation. This has contributed to a climate of suspicion in which people who have been kept in the dark about their treatment, now refuse to accept reassurance when it is given.

There is a close relationship between the drug industry and the medical profession. This has become common knowledge in recent years, making people question the impartiality of doctors. Many leading doctors and doctors' organisations such as the Royal College of Psychiatrists have links to drug companies.

There is an expectation in psychiatric hospitals that people will be given medication. It has become almost automatic. If none is prescribed it will lead to the question being asked of whether the person is really ill and really needs to be in hospital. Different drugs are indicated for different psychiatric illnesses and there are no serious psychiatric illnesses for which no drugs are indicated.

Being prepared to take medication is often interpreted as a measure of having insight and a desire to get better. There are reasons why people may prefer not to take medication, but in most psychiatric practice these are viewed with suspicion. Many people are unhappy about taking medication because they see it as a step towards giving up their own autonomy and accepting something of which they disapprove. Taking tablets to deal with mental suffering has a bad image. It is seen as weak, stupid, superficial. This is confirmed if the person gets the impression that tablets are all that they are getting. A depressed and desperate person who feels that they have been given tablets to shut them up may react with anger. To take an overdose of tablets in such circumstances is not uncommon.

The other major issue over medication concerns coercion. In the past it was expected that doctors would prescribe drugs and patients would take them. In acute psychiatry, dealing with people with serious problems in hospital, medication can be enforced - given even if the person says they do not want it. This kind of treatment is a special situation, in which an exception is made to the normal rules for obtaining consent. In the past it contributed to a tendency for psychiatric patients to be coerced into taking medication, even when their consent was lacking. This can set up an antagonism to medication, which will incline someone against it as a matter of self-assertion. The result can be that someone will not consider treatment that might in other circumstances be what they wanted. There is an easy transition from refusing to take medication because you are being forced to take it, to refusing to take any medication, on principle. Thus in a paradoxical way the over- reliance on medication can result in people not getting the benefit of it.

Electro Convulsive Therapy

This is a treatment with a terrible reputation. Many patients are frightened of the idea that they might be forced to have it. In fact it is still widely used, and doctors often act as though its public image doesn't matter. They see it as a treatment with the backing of research proving that it is helpful for certain conditions. In the Naïve Psychiatry approach; if it leads to remission of symptoms, then it must be good. The case of ECT highlights the difference between remission and recovery. If ECT is given, in spite of being feared and unwanted then the repercussions of its use are likely to far outweigh any temporary symptomatic improvement.

Doctors, who rarely or never prescribe ECT, can become defensive when challenged about it, because they feel that their position as arbiters of what is the best treatment for people is being attacked.

Compulsion

It is an inescapable fact that psychiatrists are involved in detaining and treating many of their patients against their wishes (see "The Psychiatrists Curse" Ch. 15). Throughout the time a psychiatrist is treating someone, there can be continuing discussions and debates about whether the powers of the Mental Health Act should be used. The Act remains in the background to be called upon if the psychiatrist thinks it is necessary. This legal authority to override a person's normal human rights affects the nature of the relationship. Some patients appear to be happy about it - even seeing it as a safeguard to ensure that they will be given treatment even if, at the time, they are too unwell to realise that they need it. However, such reactions are unusual and many patients have difficulty dealing with someone who they know can have them admitted to hospital against their wishes.

It might be thought that compulsion was a minor issue since in most units there are usually not more than 25% of patients detained at any one time. This figure is misleading. If 25% of current patients on a ward are detained under the Mental Health Act, then it is likely that at least another 25% have been detained at some time in the not very far distant past. Then there may be another 25% where serious discussions go on in the staff group about whether or not the person should be detained. Figures such as these were obtained in an audit that I carried out on an ordinary acute psychiatric ward. It becomes clear that being detained is a significant issue for most psychiatric patients who are treated in hospital. It is not a minor or peripheral issue.

The Expanding Medical Model

Up to now the only time that people could be forced to have psychiatric treatment has been when they were detained in hospital. Once people were discharged they regained control of their lives, and regained the right to make their own treatment decisions. The only exception was Section 41 of the Mental Health Act, which placed conditions on people's freedom for a prolonged period. This section could only be imposed by a high court and was reserved for those judged to be a serious risk to other people. There is a movement now for compulsory powers to be extended to a much larger group of people. One idea being considered would require certain patients to take medication as a condition of retaining their freedom outside hospital. This would be for people who have not committed any offence, but are thought to pose a risk.

This indicates that the Medical Model is alive and well, and accurately describes what goes on in psychiatry. One reason why psychiatrists have little patience with discussions about the Medical Model is that in the acute and stressful work that they do there seems to be no alternative. However it is only by accepting the seriousness of these objections to the Medical Model that the need to find ways to reduce its harmful effects will be accepted.

In order to broaden the concept of recovery it is necessary to understand the warfare that has gone on for many years between different theoretical viewpoints. There is a standoff with different groups thinking they are the only ones who understand things properly. It ends up as a struggle for power between different groups – with the Medical Model being supported by the leading position occupied by the medical profession. This has lead to a tyranny in which theories of many kinds completely overshadow non-scientific ways of understanding people. Before a more human concept of recovery can be developed, it has to be accepted that there are more ways of understanding people than can be fitted into randomised controlled trials, and that these are of real value, not just window dressing. The existential analysis of Laing, and the use of narrative accounts are examples of this. They show how it is necessary to dress up the blatantly obvious in fancy clothing in order to reintroduce it into this most human of subjects.

Chapter 4
THE ENDLESS DEBATE

There are many different ways that people and their mental health problems can be described. They are a series of systems of theories that have been developed independently of each other. Each tends to focus on a particular range of topics, and use its own specialised language. The different 'models' are generally used by people who share common ways of working. Examples of these are:

Models

- Medical models of mental illnesses and diagnoses.
- Psychoanalytic model focusing on unconscious mental activity
- Behavioural models emphasising learning of behaviour
- Cognitive-behavioural model, focusing on cognition and current behaviour
- Social models looking at effects of society on individuals
- Interpersonal models looking at relationships as shaping how people are
- Cultural models stressing the influence of culture on the individual
- Evolutionary models stressing role of evolution in shaping the present
- Neuro-chemical models explaining things by changes in brain chemistry

The debate between these different models has gone on for many years, and there are no signs of it being resolved. It often seems to be a tiresome, bad-tempered debate - which is not going anywhere. It might be regarded as a harmless academic matter but these disputes end up having a bad effect on how people are treated.

The models are like tracks that explorers are making into an unknown land. Each has set out from a different place around the edge, and the hope has been that one day all the maps they make can be put together to reveal what the country is really like. But the maps are all in different languages with different notations, so the grand coming together remains as far off as ever. The question always remains of how the different models relate to each other, and, if each gives a different explanation of the same things, which one is correct; or can they all be true?

Then to add to the confusion there is another series of explanations, also covering the same field. These include –

Narrative Models

Personal accounts and narratives

Case histories

Novels

Poems

Songs

Myths

These can also describe personal events in a meaningful way, but they tend to be excluded from discussions about mental health because they are not scientific.

Faced with all these ways of looking at things from different angles, the question remains of how to weigh them up. Which is the most important, or the most useful, or the truest? There are several different ways in which people approach this question, and the answers they give have a direct bearing on how they will understand recovery.

1) Scientific reductionism.

This says that in the end it will all come down to brain chemistry. At present our science is not very far advanced, which is why we have so many conflicting approaches. Once more progress has been made, neuroscience will be able to supply the answers. This is the traditional view that I was taught at school and university. It says that Psychology and Mental Health are difficult, woolly subjects that are only slowly achieving some degree of scientific respectability and emerging from the dark ages of prejudice and superstition. This view puts forwards the idea that psychology is new - because people have only started studying it in the past hundred and fifty years. It overlooks the fact that reflections on the nature of man and his place in the world are the most ancient topics of literature.

Scientific materialism used to be seen as an optimistic, simple idea that hardly needed justification. The future was onward and upwards. The transformation of the world in the twentieth century by technology was taken as an illustration of and justification for this view. To oppose it is to risk being seen as some kind of fundamentalist.

It was assumed that as scientific knowledge increased it would gradually replace older ways of explaining people and their disorders. Psychiatry was one example of the application of science to human problems. The German psychiatrist Emil Kraepelin (1856-1926) exerted a far-reaching influence with his attempt to develop a scientific way to classify mental disorders. It was he and not Freud who was the real father of modern psychiatry. The hope at the outset was that his classification would lead to the discovery of the underlying physical causes of the different mental illnesses. Once this was done it was hoped that the next stage would be the development of effective treatments.

The discovery of the cause of General Paralysis of the Insane (GPI), gave strong support to this sort of approach. GPI which was a condition characterised by personality change, psychotic symptoms, increasing weakness, memory loss and finally death. It was common in asylums in the nineteenth century, and suspicion developed that it was caused by syphilis. Finally this was proved when in 1913 Noguchi found the causative agent in the brains of patients who had died. The great hope in the early twentieth century was that similar discoveries would be made with the common forms of mental illness. However, so far, in spite of a hundred years of research, no physical causes of mental illness have been found. There have been many hopeful breakthroughs, but none have been substantiated. This has not discouraged the researchers. Techniques are always improving and the hope remains that science will come up with something, sooner or later.

The development of effective drugs to treat people with mental illness is seen as a triumph of scientific endeavour. It is hoped that once the biochemical lesions which underlie conditions such as schizophrenia are discovered, then a rational, effective treatment can be developed. In fact the drugs that have been developed so far have almost all been discovered by chance and we remain a long way off being able to design drugs to rectify specific defects. Indeed the idea of designing a drug to correct the chemical cause of an illness is just that, an idea. There is no certainty that it will be possible. Many things can be imagined and described in detail, such as moving people about by teleportation, but that doesn't mean they will ever happen.

One essential step in this research strategy is to be able to identify separate groups of people who have similar psychiatric problems. It is hoped that such problems will be caused by the same biochemical abnormality. The existence and stability of separable groups - as diagnostic categories - is thus vital for work in psychopharmacology.

The great growth of this work has required and supported the Neo-Kraepelinianism (N-K) of recent decades. The N-K approach has seen a resurgence of interest in classifying patients into clearly defined illness groupings. The DSM and ICD classifications have gone from being research instruments to being part of the language of psychiatry. The illness concepts were given detailed operational definitions in an attempt to standardise classification. Diagnostic groupings, which were justified as aids to research have acquired lives of their own. What began as tentative hypotheses are being treated by up and coming generations of psychiatrists as real entities – diseases.

By this process mental illnesses are now much more clearly defined than in the past. Some people still argue that mental illnesses do no exist. However, they are concepts that have been defined in such a way that they can be applied to the people who present with mental health problems. A better question is not whether they exist, but whether they are useful concepts, and how much individuals benefit from having a diagnosis made.

The reductionist scientific answer to the competing models is that it is simply a matter of time until science is able to come up with a unifying theory. At present there are many different sciences which study man from different angles but once neuroscience is sufficiently advanced, neurochemistry will provide the ultimate explanation. To go back to the analogy of the different explorers, once neuroscience is sufficiently advanced it will take over and colonise the whole area.

2) Paradigms in Conflict

Thomas Kuhn in "The Structure of Scientific Revolutions" (1962) produced a different way of explaining the seemingly intractable conflicts between different approaches. He described a paradigm as an entire system of study, research and the advancement of knowledge. One would become involved by being educated and then working within an approach; so that one would learn to judge... One would learn to judge any piece of work by the standards that one had acquired during one's education and academic apprenticeship. Within the paradigm there will be significant pieces of work that are leading examples of good science. Textbooks have an important place in gathering approved findings and methods. They also help to mark out the areas of interest to people working within a particular paradigm. Orthodox science will go on within the paradigm, with the results having clear relevance to the existing findings. To those working within a paradigm, work going on outside will not be of great interest. It may not be seen as science at all.

It is suggested that different paradigms exist, with workers not crossing boundaries from one to another. The work carried out under different paradigms may relate to the same general area - such as influences on people's behaviour - but the topics studied will be different. The paradigm is an expression of a particular social and cultural group, so that in a particular society at a particular time, a certain paradigm may have a dominating position. The relative positions of different paradigms will be decided not by the settling of arguments by scientific experiments, but by the power relationships of groups within society.

This view fits in with many features of the mental health scene. Orthodox scientific psychiatry is part of the dominant scientific paradigm. It finds expression in a large literature base, which focuses on its own chosen topics. There is a large industry producing research. Over 1 billion dollars is spent on psychiatric research in the US each year. There are rigorous training schemes to ensure that those entering the field have been inducted into the correct paradigm. To qualify as a psychiatrist you have to subscribe to certain core beliefs. You have to accept the value of medication to treat schizophrenia, and that treatment decisions should be influenced by randomised controlled trials.

The Kuhn type of explanation is interesting as a generality, and can explain the surprising lack of communication between different groups in the same field, but is less easy to apply in detail. It is not clear how one could decide how many paradigms there are, and it is not true that workers in different paradigms are never influenced by work going on outside. It could be argued that much of the best work goes on in the grey areas between established fields of study.

The notion of paradigms does help to explain why nobody gets won over by research. It is true that many workers stay in a narrow area, being interested in a particular group of problems. Those problems may never be solved and interest in them may die with that generation of researchers who have devoted their lives to them. Devoted their lives, but also derived their life and their livelihoods from them.

3) Postmodernism.

This is another version of the "different paradigms" model, but putting the matter in a wider cultural context (Bracken P. and Thomas P. 2001). It is not just a question of differing "schools of thought" or "academic disciplines", it concerns different cultures and systems of belief in people who may be living next to each other in contemporary western society. It is claimed that there is no longer a consensus about how people should live, or what might constitute a good life. This is highlighted in a multicultural society, where the customs and traditions of different groups do not share common assumptions. It is also a result of the great increase in individual autonomy and rights that has occurred in the past fifty years. It may well be that society has always contained within it a number of subgroups with their own distinct identity. In the past they were inhibited or even prohibited from expressing their diversity. There is now a positive celebration of diversity. It is no longer expected that the there will be single prevailing culture to which all must subscribe in order to be regarded as normal.

The concept of postmodernism questions the idea that there can be scientifically established criteria of what it is to recover. It will all depend on what is accepted within the culture within which someone is living. Psychology – as a discipline – tends to come with its own cultural assumptions - which are generally those of white, liberal, upwardly mobile westerners. The cultural expectations of this group are in conflict with many traditions. This conflict is often presented not as difference between different cultures, but as the difference between science and ignorance. This perspective adds further support to the idea that what constitutes recovery must take account of the individual's culture and aspirations.

4) A Wittgensteinian Analysis of the Problem

Wittgenstein was one of the most influential philosophers of the twentieth century, and in the second half of his career he devoted a lot of his time to the philosophy of mind. He was a revolutionary thinker who attempted to deal with problems that have troubled philosophers since the time of the ancient Greeks. He tried to understand how it is that certain problems can go on provoking theorising and debate for centuries but never come close to being solved. He called into question the idea that psychology is a young science that just needs more time and better experiments to sort out the problems. Instead he suggested that people have been studying the problems of psychology for a very long time, but have been confused. His famous quote is that " *in psychology there are experimental methods and conceptual confusions ...The existence of the experimental method makes us think we have the means of solving the problems which trouble us; though problem and method pass one another by."* Wittgenstein said that philosophical problems arise through misuse of language. People were trying to answer questions that looked as though they were questions asking for information, when in fact they arose from conceptual confusion. The solution then was not to come up with a theory, or an answer, but to understand better how the confusion arose. It was more a question of diagnosing the cause of the problem in logic rather than producing yet another theory.

Another of Wittgenstein's sayings, which he said could have been a motto for his later work was - *"I will show you differences"*. He was saying that much of the confusion over psychology comes from people wanting to generalise, wanting to group things together so that they can develop a broad theory. This he saw as a particular failing when people talk about psychology. The word itself suggests a science or a discipline, whereas in fact psychology is simply a grouping together of lots of different ways of studying people; like the different explorers each making their separate journeys in the unknown land.

It is difficult to grasp the message of a philosopher who did not believe in theories. He worked in a rigorous way, with examples being dissected in great detail. He came to see doing philosophy as carrying out a special kind of intellectual inquiry. He sought to pass on his method, and his attitude, rather than a body of findings.

Although mental phenomena and the area generally covered by psychology was one of his major interests, his direct influence on that field has been limited. Psychology has moved a long way in the fifty years since he was writing, and it has come to occupy a much more central place in western culture. This means that the errors which he saw as infecting academic discussions are now very much part of our culture. His warnings about the confusion caused by seeing psychology as a science are more relevant today than ever.

Psychiatry was a subject to which Wittgenstein had a curious attraction. He had great misgivings about the idea of being a professional philosopher and was not convinced that it was a worthwhile way to spend one's life. One of his pupils, Maurice Drury, who became a close friend, was persuaded by Wittgenstein to abandon a career in academic philosophy and to take up medicine and later psychiatry. He himself seems to have considered the idea of training to be a psychiatrist (Monk 1990). Drury (1973) talks about the dangers of psychological theorising making people think they know more than they really do. It is of interest that the type of psychiatry that Drury describes is an empirically based, practical and pragmatic approach to 'getting people better'. He was one of the first generation of psychiatrists to see dramatic results from physical treatments in the 1950's and'60's. From his writing he sounds remarkably like a follower of William Sargant!

A Wittgensteinian diagnosis of the debates over psychiatry could begin by pointing out that psychiatry is an odd sort of thing. It is the name of a profession, but not of an activity. There are lots of different things that may be done by a psychiatrist, but these are not psychiatry. There are other activities done by other people within psychiatric institutions or psychiatric teams, and each of these has some connection to psychiatry. An occupational therapist helping someone regain confidence after a spell in hospital might take all referrals from a psychiatric team, but might not call what they were doing psychiatric treatment. A nurse looking after a disturbed patient on a ward may have mental health training, but might not call what s/he does psychiatric treatment.

Psychiatry is a wide area and it would be impossible to find any single way of linking together all the things that go on. They all have things in common, but no one thing. They have what Wittgenstein called a *"family resemblance"*. This means that there is no way that the things that get called psychiatry can be brought under a single theory. There will be generalisations that can be made about parts of the field, but not about the whole.

If psychiatry is not an activity or a method for doing anything there will be no gain from trying to put together a single theory or model. There will be many different generalisations that can be made about specific situations. Drury was an advocate of ECT, and other physical treatments. He describes dramatic improvements produced by these agents and he was clearly impressed. However he was not putting forwards any theory about it.

In the years since he was practising, theory has come to have a dominating influence in the field of mental health.

A psychiatry that does not put forwards broad general theories can look rather lacklustre and humdrum. It is not going to become an exclusive sect that is interesting to join. It does not even have a name. It is interesting that there was a psychiatrist, as eminent as Kraepelin or Freud in his day, who put forward an approach something like this: Adolph Meyer (1866-1949). However, because the breadth and humanity of his work did not lend itself to scientific elaboration, his reputation and even his name are now largely forgotten (Gelder M. 1991). A difficulty in the present discussion is that theories are being debated, and points raised, but no general theory will emerge. If there is any simple conclusion it is that overgeneralisation and the illusion that in dealing with people we have general "scientific" principles to fall back on, are the greatest dangers. We now suffer from the tyranny of theories.

The Tyranny of Theories

The models that have been developed in mental health started from humble beginnings. They began with some simple intervention which was thought to be helpful, maybe a particular way of giving advice, a drug being prescribed or a plan of action to combat a symptom or problem. From the idea that the intervention was helpful came the thought that this must mean that understanding how the treatment worked will throw light on how the problem developed in the first place. So if the drug was known to lower a particular chemical in the brains of experimental animals, then maybe the problem was caused by that chemical being too high in the first place – in humans. If talking about an upsetting event has been helpful, then maybe it was not being able to talk about it that caused the problem.

Each of these bits of theorising involves large measures of speculation and major leaps of the imagination. It also remains an open question whether the treatments that were the starting points for the theories really produced the improvements claimed, and if they did, what was the active ingredient.

Once a theory has taken root it assumes a life of its own. It gets developed into an elaborate system, which convincingly explains a wide range of problems. A model that worked well when explaining the effects of a particular type of intervention is stretched to cover the whole field. The concepts are clear and simple – as they are derived from a limited number of observations and so have the great advantage of being objective and therefore measurable. Science can then be done and results obtained which are objective - free of the subjectivity of personal experience. These approaches are reductive in the sense that they reduce down the complexity of human experience to one or two basic principles.

The models derived in this way tend to be supported most strongly by those professionals whose work provided the original observations on which the theory is based. Therefore professional rivalries are expressed in competition between the different theories. Psychiatrists, psychologists, social workers, and many varieties of psychotherapists will all in their training have been exposed to different theoretical approaches. This is not a bad thing and is inevitable. As a trainee, one needs clear guidelines, ways to organise the complex material in the field. Teaching would be impossible if there were no principles by which to arrange the facts. One gains confidence by being able to make sense of the situations that occur. The simplicity of theories is a great attraction at the outset.

Trainees in mental health face a daunting situation. At the time that they start they are usually young, and have had limited life experience. They may never have encountered distress or grief or mental disturbance, and will be conscious of their own anxieties. Once they start work they will meet people who are in disturbed states, people who are asking for help and advice, and answers. There is an immediate need to be able to make sense of the distress. The part-theories then have great attraction. They are sim-plifications of complex and intractable problems. They provide people with guidance on how to act, what to do – and in this they are very successful. It is remarkable to see a novice psychiatrist, with only a few months' experience, go into an alarming situation and be able to restore some semblance of calm. The conviction with which the newcomer can make decisions about other people's lives is remarkable, but also alarming.

Thus, simple models are necessary to help people find their way in a difficult field,and are effective in helping people carry out difficult jobs.

They work well for the jobs for which they are devised. However they develop lives of their own - way beyond the narrow area of their inception. They get expanded to provide explanations for all kinds of psychological problems, and also normal psychological functioning. Because the theories are derived from a few simple ideas, they can develop into closed systems, which will answer any question that comes up. The theory may become complex and convoluted; yet still retain its ability to convince people by its internal logic. So – simple theories tend to expand to cover the whole field, explaining all of human life. They are very convincing to those that follow them, and give those who are initiated into them a dangerous sense of certainty. They are enemies of humility in the face of uncertainty. People come to believe that their theories are true: they are not seen as useful ways of looking at things, or working hypotheses, but as true, genuine insights into what people are really like. This is where the tyranny starts. It means that one person can tell another what is really true for them. It means that one very partial way of looking at things is taken as real.

Thirty-five years ago when I was student of psychology it was a very dull subject. Most researchers had concluded that the really interesting things about people were too difficult for science. This resulted in a whole generation of academic psychologists spending their time doing experiments on rats running in mazes, or pressing levers to get food. It was only the behaviour of such creatures that could be studied in what was then believed to be a scientific way. These studies of various animals, in totally artificial situations, resulted in mechanistic theories which were then extrapolated to explain how people live their lives. And then from those theories ways of treating people with mental disorders were developed. The theories gained credibility because they were based on what, at the time was regarded as "hard science".

This process has also occurred with recovery. A narrow (scientifically acceptable) approximation for recovery has come to dominate the field. Scientific studies by their nature have to be reductive; they have to focus on a limited number of quantifiable aspects of the situation. Studies of recovery involve measures of symptoms and of function. They are called measures, but even this is an analogy rather than a precise way of talking. One cannot measure most symptoms because they are subjective experiences. What can be studied are statements made by people who are asked questions by researchers. The answers are then rated according to agreed scales.

The large number of reductive models which are used within the mental health field give the impression that every angle is being covered. If one does not favour a biochemical approach, then you can add in a sociological one. If that is not enough, then an interpersonal perspective can be added. Psychiatrists are irritated by criticisms of the "Medical Model". It is thought to imply that they are only interested in physical, organic or genetic factors. They will counter this by explaining that modern psychiatry uses a very broad eclectic approach, which can accommodate every shade of opinion within it.   All this talk of different models convinces many professionals that the ways they have of understanding their patients are now both broad and deep. Surely, it is argued, all aspects of human life are covered, psychiatry should not still be accused of operating along narrow medical lines. Yet this forgets the limitations of all these theoretical approaches. They all began as generalisations from small areas of work. They are vast edifices build on tiny foundations. They all take account of the need to be scientific; neutral and detached. They all start from the idea of observing people from the outside, and building a science from what is seen. They lack the concept of a person making their own decisions. Models are needed to inform decision-making about aspects of treatment, but the psychology that comes across bears little relation to real people taking control of their lives.

The scientific, detached viewpoint imposes a degree of helplessness and anonymity. It is a picture of people, made vulnerable by their past experiences, facing an uncertain future in which they will undoubtedly suffer more. The illusion that comes from the multi-model, multidimensional assessment of psychiatric patients is that here is a science that can explain people. It is assumed that the various models will one day come together to produce a joined up scientific explanation that will cover every aspect of people's lives. The imperialism of neuroscience assumes that one day it will conquer all. Yet "There are more things in heaven and earth, Horatio, than are dreamed of in your philosophy," as Shakespeare put it. There is more to people than can be captured by observing them from outside, and there is no joining up of the different models.

There is a pervasive myth that it is only through science that we can get to understand people properly. It is said to provide a truer, deeper perspective - which is essential if one is to be able to help anyone. Non-scientific ways of describing people may be interesting and colourful and poetic and many other things that are all very well in their own place: but when it comes to helping people who are really ill, science must take the lead. This is an assumption that would be justified if science was providing the total picture it claims. It comes decisively unstuck on the subject of recovery. The ways of describing experience paying more attention to the personal and concerned with people's individual narratives turn out to be vital if one is to help people steer their own personal course towards recovery. This unscientific approach is how people make sense of their own lives and those of others.

Chapter 5
NARRATIVES AND HUMAN EXISTENCE

Attempts to describe and explain human experience are not limited to science. If reductive scientific accounts are felt to be lacking in some way, then there are narrative ways of describing the human condition.

Existential Writers

Existentialism is an old-fashioned word, suggesting something impenetrable to British common sense. People don't talk about it any more. The British knew enough to suspect that there was something earnest and serious about it, something slightly foreign and unnecessary. In the 1960's when I first encountered existentialism it appeared revolutionary and subversive. It did not fit into the world as I encountered it. Since then, by a process of gradual osmosis, all that has changed. Without anyone noticing it, the existential view has come to exert a powerful influence in our culture. Many have deplored and resisted this change which they see as giving us a world obsessed with self. This view is now the prevailing way that we understand other people but it has not been taken seriously by writers concerned with mental health.

The existential view produced a sea change elevating the importance of the individual experience. The world around has come to be seen as lacking in meaning and value, and individuals now have the task of creating and seeking out meaning in the world for themselves. This is the world in which religious, class and political affiliations have all come to be seen as optional interests for minority groups. Iconoclasm has lost its appeal to the young - because the old icons, which earlier generations came to find oppressive - have all been destroyed or marginalised. The existential writers opened this up. It was a struggle - as they were challenging beliefs and structures that they had been brought up to respect. Those born later find it difficult to appreciate the anguish of the struggle, because those old beliefs no longer exert their influence.

It is paradoxical that those earlier writers who created the modern world get overlooked and forgotten. After all - what they were saying now seems so obvious it no longer seems a hard won insight. The changed view of man probably has fairly little to do with the branch of philosophy called existentialism. The changes in the world that produced our modern consciousness also produced existentialism, which was an early expression of it. Philosophy is very much a minority interest, but the changes in our views on 'being a person' are being expressed in a wide range of popular cultural activities.

In the 50's and 60's psychology had less hold on popular culture than it does now. It was still a small specialised subject - though one with a long tradition of writing on alternative, life-style issues. There were popularisations of psychoanalysis, exotic religions and self-improvement theories, which tended to be sold in small specialist bookshops to a self-consciously eccentric clientele.

The publication of "*The Outsider*" by Colin Wilson in 1956 was a brief moment when existential ideas were put forward in a popular book, which became a best seller in Britain. It is a strange book; even stranger when reread nearly fifty years later. Wilson wrote the book when he was twenty-four. He was an autodidact who spent his days reading in the British Museum Reading Room, and his nights sleeping on Hampstead Heath. When the book was published he became an overnight celebrity. The book was cobbled together from notebooks that Wilson had made during his wide-ranging reading. He made extensive use of quotations from other writers – novelists, diarists and philosophers. The extracts that he chose were narratives that described individual experience. It was people reflecting on their experience and trying to make sense of it. They were describing what it was like to be an individual, reflecting, private person; that is, a person who is not defined by their job, or their family position, or their predicament, or by any other incidental contingent feature.

The book gives a strong impression of showing something, but it is not clear what that is. The title of the book - *The Outsider* - is misleading. It sets up the expectation that the book is about a particular type of person, or even a disorder. It may be that at the time the writer did feel that that was what he was doing. There is no clearly developed theory in the book. It was rather that he was trying to show or illustrate something.

What really comes across is not a description of a type of person, but a position or point of view. It is the detached "outside looking in" view. Some people may rarely occupy this position. If they are very busy, taken up with the things of the world, they may never pause long enough to develop the detached outsider's view. If a person has a set of strong beliefs, which explain and account for most of what they see, then their worldview will lack the mystery and strangeness that Wilson was describing. One key ingredient for his position was a degree of detachment. This requires time on one's own, time to think. It may be enhanced by physical detachment. It also requires a lack of belief, an agnosticism about what is going on.

These conditions must apply to a large proportion of serious writers - which is why Wilson's examples are so widely scattered. One gets the impression that he could have quoted from any book he had read. This result is odd - at first he seems to be describing a particular type of person, but then most of the people who have written about themselves turn out to be examples of his description. The conclusion appears to be that in so far as we contemplate the world from a detached, neutral position we are all outsiders. Yet, at the time, this was an interesting observation.

One problem with the message Wilson was trying to get across is that it is too simple. It all depends on adopting a certain attitude. It involves taking seriously one's experience - as experience, and not focusing all the time on the content. There is no hard information to impart, no real news. The problems faced by the people in Wilson's literary examples, are problems that many people face today. They are not even problems, more predicaments. So it is always open for someone to respond by saying, "So what? It is all so obvious it is not worth saying. All serious thinkers have always known this": or to quote T.S.Eliot –"That is not it at all. That is not what I meant, at all."

One way to take the original insight further is to develop it into an elaborate philosophy. It is possible to invent many new concepts to describe this viewpoint. It can then be dissected and analysed, and compared with other ways of understanding the world. This has tended to happen whenever psychiatrists become interested in philosophy. That there is some important insight is obvious, but pretty soon an impenetrable thicket of jargon grows up around it so that only those who have spent years studying the subject can understand what is being said. This happened to existentialism, which is now strictly not for the general reader.

Wilson did not go down that route. He has continued to explore human experience in all its weird diversity in the dozens of books he has written. He has maintained an unfashionable interest on how life can be transformed by what he calls "peak experiences", times when people feel everything more intensely than normal. This explains why he has come to occupy a place as an eccentric literary outsider (to use the word in its more ordinary way).

I mention Wilson because he was certainly significant for me, and I think his contribution is forgotten. It is interesting that the kinds of artistic work that he highlighted have become ever more popular. One reason that his contribution is ignored is that the positive optimistic message of his later work is so much out of fashion. He may one day be recognised as a pioneer of positive psychology.

The case of R.D.Laing has more obvious relevance to how people with mental disorders are understood. He came to prominence a few years later than Wilson, and he followed a different route. He was a precocious boy who showed early brilliance at school. He began with an interest in classics and although studying medicine, he maintained a preoccupation with philosophy. He had an early ambition to become famous and make his name. Like many other innovators he had that ambition before he had settled on the field that he was going to follow.

Laing followed the recognised career path for someone who wants to be a psychiatrist. He was developing his ideas in the 1950's, and is said to have been annoyed that Wilson was able to publish his book before him and at such a young age. He published "*The Divided Self*" in 1960, and this made his name, not overnight like "*The Outsider*", but over a few years. The book was on the subject of schizophrenia, viewed from an existential perspective. He was mixing concepts from psychoanalysis and continental philosophy to give weight and credibility to his personal view of psychiatry. He had worked as a psychiatrist while doing his National Service in the army, but by 1957 when the book was finished, he was still very new to the field. He brought together several different types of writing.

Firstly, the book has all the trappings of a heavyweight psychoanalytic treatise from the Tavistock Clinic. It was published by the Tavistock Press and in the preface Laing acknowledges the "encouragement and helpful criticism" that he had received from a long list of eminent figures in the psychoanalytic establishment.

Secondly it seeks to break new ground by starting with an account of "existential - phenomenology". This uses concepts from existential philosophy to explain the person's relationship to the world. Then he goes on to describe "ontological insecurity" as a condition in which the individual's relation to the world is fundamentally flawed.

Thirdly Laing included a series of case histories. These were narratives of young people, disjointed from their own lives and from those around them, but described with great sympathy.

Fourthly, he wrote personal accounts of his experiences as an army doctor. He felt much more sympathy for the so-called schizophrenic patients than he did with the system within which he was working. He also critically dissected a passage from Kraepelin. In this he again sides with the patient who was being presented at a case conference in a way that was degrading and humiliating. He shows that any conclusions drawn from viewing people in that way are bound to be suspect and wrong. This fourth strand of the argument fits in with the movement that had already started to challenge the way that the mentally ill were treated and understood (e.g. Foudraine, 1974). It goes further than most in showing that not only was the system morally corrupt, but also that it would inevitably support false theories about the mentally ill.

One of the claims of the book was that Laing could communicate with and understand the mentally ill. He advocated a kind of careful listening, which would reveal meaning where a superficial medical history taking could discover only nonsense. "The Divided Self" became very popular in the 1960's. It appealed beyond those who were interested in schizophrenia to a much wider readership trying to understand themselves. The case histories were striking stories, written from the inside. They describe people detached from and threatened by their surroundings. They are reminiscent of "The Outsider" accounts quoted by Wilson. They rang true to the young people who read them, describing experiences that they could relate to. The power of the writing must have come from the strong personal feelings of the writer. Laing later revealed that one of the histories was based on himself and his family, confirming that these were more than just clinical case histories. He was writing something intensely personal, and his non-specialist readers picked this up. If after reading Wilson we are all "Outsiders", after reading Laing we are all "Schizophrenics"

There were many different messages in Laing's writings, so that different people could go away with different things. There can be no way of saying that one message was the real or true one. However I think that two major legacies can be seen flowing from his work. One is of great and lasting importance, and has not been stated better or more clearly by anyone since his time. This is his existential understanding of the individual, and his awareness of the moral conflicts in the mental health field. This legacy has been obscured and squandered by the greater prominence of the second legacy. This was his support for a range of specific models and therapies, which I regard as mostly misguided and harmful in their effects.

Laing came up against a paradox that lies at the heart of the idea of therapy and psychiatry. He came across people suffering from great mental distress. He recognised that they were having difficulty making themselves understood, and that knaves and fools were taking advantage of them. He found that by taking time and listening carefully he could help to sort something out. Everyone was very impressed and those in distress appeared genuinely better off. So he started to explain to people what he did. He borrowed ideas from psychology, sociology, philosophy and any other 'ology' that might throw light on the matter. The problem now was that he was back where he started, except that now he was the teacher of the knaves and fools. He began to believe his own complex theories and this, in the end, obscured his original insight.

Laing became associated in the public mind with the theory that schizophrenia is caused by families. He also espoused various specific forms of therapy as the answer to what was needed to help people. He remained part of the medical profession, but for an innovative psychiatrist his philosophical and ethical ideas were not enough to establish his position. Within the medical model it is necessary to come up with a clever new treatment in order to make your name. This Laing attempted with various new ideas. The final ones were LSD therapy, and analysis for pre-natal trauma. These crazy ideas would have finished his career if his own self-destructive behaviour had not got there first. He ended up discredited and on the point of being struck off the medical register for unprofessional behaviour.

The manner of the ending of Laing's career enabled the psychiatric profession to disregard what he had been saying. This was difficult for many psychiatrists, me included, as his early example had been so inspiring. Recently there has been a slight resurgence of interest in Laing. Historians and philosophers have begun reclaiming bits of his legacy. They still tend to avoid the existential-ethical dimension. Laing was locked into the medical model - he was looking for a break-through, a clever idea that would make his name. He was attracted to theories that would explain people, and explain how to put them right; on the look out for the brilliant idea that would resolve the problems of mental suffering at a stroke. He was waiting for the "card that is so high and wild he'll never need to deal another". But he never found one. He failed in those endeavours because his ideas were not very good and did not work, and because that whole quest for a simple solution is doomed anyway. That quest is the snare and delusion on which most psychiatric innovators have foundered. Laing's other legacy was an inspiration to a generation of workers in mental health, and needs to be revived.

The existential insight is that you will only get in touch with people if you learn to listen to them: listening without categorising or judging, and accepting the moral imperative not to harm people by jumping to conclusions. He was saying that what people say about their own experience has more validity than any number of medical diagnoses. This is a simple message, too simple for a subject like psychiatry, which is based on analysing and dissecting things - and always going beyond what is there on the surface. It is also difficult for psychiatrists to be genuinely impartial listeners because of the "psychiatrists curse", their unique responsibility to step in and rescue people, if their mental disorder places them at risk, (see Ch 15).

The ethical message was that people who are affected by mental disorder are still people and as worthy of respect as anyone else. This was at a time when the mentally ill were regarded as non-people, with no status in society at all. Laing was not the only person standing up for the basic humanity of the mentally ill, but he was the most prominent and charismatic.

Wilson and Laing were both inspired by the existential world view. They each became celebrities by putting forward a striking new vision of people and how they are in the world. That vision is now taken for granted in today's culture. The very acceptance of what they were saying has contributed to their eclipse. Literature and the arts are filled with images reflecting this. However the mental health field has lagged behind. Here a view persists that the only way to understanding is through reductive science which allows things to be counted and submitted to statistical analysis. The understanding gained from narrative accounts of people's lives is relegated to a peripheral place - as merely anecdotal.

Case Histories

Freud's writings have remained attractive to a wide readership – and much of this must come down to his case histories. He describes patients who he treated, but does so in a way that is more like the story-telling of a novelist, than the dry-as-dust reporting of a scientist. He describes real people, as he encountered them. It is not surprising that many writers have adapted this technique for their own creative works and "pretend case histories" are now a genre of fiction in their own right.

Many other writers on psychiatric topics make liberal use of case histories. These may be presented as examples or illustrations. In fact, it is the case histories that carry the information and real content of the work. Further evidence for this comes from the large literature of self-help books. These are written specifically for people who want to understand their own condition. They are a critical audience who have no time for vague generalities. Such books are good at giving vivid accounts of what it is like to suffer from mental health problems. The narratives allow identification with others. They also convey hope and advice. The emotional effect of reading narratives derives from the fact that the person understands. They are no longer alone and isolated in their suffering. This phenomenon is of great significance in the process of recovery. It depends upon the impact of forms of knowledge and understanding ignored by science.

Reading about other people's experiences, similar to what one is going through oneself, turns out to be remarkably helpful. Narrative accounts have a central place in how we understand other people (Roberts & Holmes 1999), and whatever theories we construct are secondary to that understanding. There is a case for saying that narratives of lives are not reducible without loss: loss of meaning: loss of truth to reality. A person without a history would not be a real person at all. It is of great significance that the general public, with all their leisure and access to the media, tend to choose to spend a lot of their time watching, listening to, or reading narratives of people's lives. That is how people instinctively seek to understand others.

This is not the way of science. There it is necessary to break things down and study small incidents, short periods of time. One reason for this is that it is easier to study small things. It is also simpler if things are studied in isolation, away from their context. The study of abstracted small elements can lead to scientific theories because simple patterns emerge and predictions can be made. The selected item can then be regarded as something scientists know about. However there is great consternation because when studied "in the wild" the simple rules are rarely followed.

It is often said by psychiatrists that they learn more about human nature from the great novelists than from all the psychiatric writers put together. There is explicit recognition of this by the Royal College of Psychiatrists which puts out a list of recommended novels for trainees to read. However it is never clear whether such talk is really meant to be taken seriously. Quotations from novelists do not feature in psychiatric reports. They do not provide any concrete advice about how to cope with particular types of problem. So is this just window dressing: the profession trying to humanise its image, getting away from the unpopular "Medical Model"?

David Lodge (2002) has written about the conflict between scientific and narrative ways of describing people in his essay *"Consciousness and the Novel"*. He makes the point that science and the novel are trying to do different things. Science tries to formulate general explanatory laws, which will apply universally. These laws were there, waiting to be discovered, they are a fixed aspect of the world. Literature on the other hand describes the "dense specificity of personal experience", which is always unique, because each of us has a different personal history. In the novel, accounts are able to follow the unique experience of individuals. Narrative literature is able to represent the density of events that are consciously experienced, and so create models of what it is like to be a human being, moving through time and space. In this way narrative is not some second-rate homely account, to be disregarded once science has caught up. It is the closest we can come to the unknowable reality of the experience of other people. A fascinating part of Lodge's thesis is that consciousness, as we know it now, here, in our culture, is changing and developing. The novel has played a significant part in the story so far, and media of the future will contribute to continuing the process.

If science and narrative do different things; some of what we come across in mental health clearly needs scientific analysis, other things need narrative description. The understanding of people and their journeys to recovery is a matter for narrative. The application of specific treatments to improve a person's mental state involves a lot of science. The confusion of these different areas is the subject of this book.

Chapter 6
COPING WITH MENTAL ILLNESS

The Naïve View

The simplified medical view of mental illness has always stressed the importance of being a good patient. This required education about the nature of the illness and about how the treatment works. There was much emphasis on giving information as a way of ensuring cooperation. The information is usually over-simplified and given with an air of authority, as though difficult questions such as 'what is the cause of schizophrenia?' have agreed answers. The aim seems to have been to provide people with a useful and correct attitude with which to face their problems. It is a bit like issuing a phrase book to someone in a foreign country; in fact information for patients often contains 'answers to questions you are likely to ask'.

The problem with this kind of help is that it is too intellectual, and the reactions of the person to what has happened to them can get left out. The message is that treatment should remove the illness, so you don't need to focus on that but on cooperating with treatment and getting better. The experience of being driven mad by the most extraordinary things happening to you, and then dragged into hospital and treated against your will is not relevant to a naïve view. 'Recovery' in a naïve view involves putting all those bad thoughts out of your mind; after all they are all unreal. Denial was very much part of the old recovery model; and fits in with traditional British ideas of what a person should be. At the time when Sargant and others were establishing the "naïve psychiatry" model, stoicism and understatement were seen as ideal characteristics. Sargant, the bluff rugby playing Englishman of the old school, was typical of the well-meaning paternalists developing the new psychiatry. Their concept of a person was the one that was current at that time. It was taken for granted, and it is only now, looking back from fifty years on, that it is clear how much things have changed. At that time there was much emphasis on conformity in society, and it was more reasonable to assume that recovery meant getting back to how you were. Recovery meant once again being an efficient, uncomplaining member of society, being able to fit in. A gradual change has occurred in the concept of what it is to be a person, and this is very relevant to the development of ideas about recovery. Today it is assumed that people will be affected by the experiences that they have and coping with their reactions will be as important as losing their symptoms.

Effects on self-image

To be vigorous healthy and generally acceptable is what young people want. That is how people try to present themselves to others. That is what you need to be in order to get on in life. Children compete from an early age, and blemishes of any kind are quickly picked up and exploited. Images of physical perfection exert a powerful influence. The attempt to measure up to what is expected causes many to develop problems such as depression, substance abuse or eating disorders. In a similar way there is great pressure to be normal from a mental point of view. Being normal is a desperately desirable commodity. However, being normal can come to be seen as an impossible goal. It means not being distinctive, not deviating from the norm in any conspicuous area. The ability to form relationships and be at ease with other people is an area where many, especially those with autistic tendencies, have difficulties. These problems may cause personal distress and loneliness, though many will not complain of that. More suffering is caused by the perception of being different, any particular difference may be often ridiculed in the media. A large percentage of funny people portrayed in comedy are being ridiculed because they are awkward, different and unable to fit in. Some of this may be seen as friendly and inclusive, but most is not.

It is well known that children from a young age will taunt each other with any insult that comes to hand. The accusation of being "mental" is very common, often followed by the idea that the person needs treatment, or needs to "go somewhere". In Cheshire when I was growing up it was ' The Deva' at Chester with which children slandered each other. We knew nothing about the place or what went on there, but still to be someone who had to go there was the worst thing we could imagine. This kind of thinking has been prevalent for generations, and has played a part in the negative stereotypes of people with mental health problems. Similar ideas are often voiced by adults who say things like "You need treatment" or "are you still taking the tablets?". Jokes about "care in the community", show how prejudice against people with mental health problems is keeping up with developments in the field. The stigmatisation of mental abnormality is universal and probably felt most acutely by the young. As people grow up in such a culture they will apply the stigma to their own self when a mental health problem develops.

It is against this background that people, usually young people, first become aware that there is something wrong. Symptoms, complaints, problems develop - things which do not fit into the scheme of things. The tendency to denial is very great. It is encouraged by the fact that most early symptoms are private and deniable. Maybe they will go away, maybe everyone feels like this but doesn't say.

The reactions of the self to the suspicion that they are suffering from mental illness are complex and often contradictory. Fear and anxiety are common. They may be due to the uncertainty of the situation. It is easy for someone to jump to conclusions. Their thinking may have settled on very negative, pessimistic conclusions before they get to the stage of confiding in someone. They may have decided that they are "losing their mind", or "going completely insane", and that nothing can be done about it. The perception of damage to ones self can set off strong negative and potentially self-destructive reactions. All the negative connotations of mental illness will now be applied by the person to him or her self.

Society sets great store by being successful, and being seen to be successful. People work steadily from childhood onwards to perfect one thing – their own self, and an image that they can present to the world. The onset or the awareness of the onset of mental illness can put all this in jeopardy. The emotions that are generated cause anxiety, depression, substance abuse or suicide. The suicide rate in young intelligent men who develop schizophrenia is about twenty percent. These tend to be people who kill themselves, not at the height of acute mental disturbance (although of course that can happen), but when they are quite lucid, and apparently improving. It is not the psychosis that is killing them but their reaction to it.

The impact of psychotic symptoms

The positively identifiable symptoms of psychosis such as hallucinations, disorders of thinking and loss of a sense of the self, may in themselves be terrifying. The person who goes through this may be overwhelmed by powerful and strange experiences that they find difficult to put into words. Psychotic thinking may be intermittent, with the person having some awareness that something is wrong. If they do try to explain to someone what has been happening, they may be misunderstood. They may be discouraged from talking of such things, told that they have misunderstood what is happening to them, or told not to worry because it is something that lots of people get, and they will soon get better. Or the experiences may be persistent, with the person trapped in a waking nightmare in which terrible things happen, and from which there is no escape.

If this kind of thing goes on for any length of time it leaves deep scars. There may be a persisting difficulty accounting for what has happened. There may be a preoccupation and fascination with the strange things that have been experienced. There may be re-runs in which some of the fearful things return - but now with more awareness of what is going on. Many people will become obsessed with trying to make sense of it all.

After-effects

To all this mental trauma there is added another layer which for many is worse that the first. This is made up of the experience of being treated for mental illness. The fears and misinterpretations can easily be compounded by the effect of being detained, admitted to hospital against your will and then forced to accept medical treatments. The situation in many acute psychiatric wards is very frightening. Professionals get used to the situation, hardened to it, but someone coming in to it for the first time can be quite traumatised. A post-traumatic state has been described in which people have difficulty getting over the experiences that occur during their first episodes of psychosis and their treatment.

Depression is a common reaction to this situation. There is a bitter grief at the perception that the future that they were hoping for is now impossible. The person's aspirations and opportunities seem to have been snatched away. This may all have been thought through in private, and the first that other people may know of anything wrong may be when the person attempts to take their own life. Grief and loss may affect someone at the outset, but may continue to trouble them for a long time. Post-psychotic depression occurs in about half of those with first episodes, and is linked to the perception of personal loss and damage. It is a grief that is difficult to deal with, partly because it is difficult to express. It runs counter to the simple medical model to talk of grief and loss. If the focus is all on getting treatment right so that you can get back to normal, then grieving will be for ever put off. Grieving implies a degree of acceptance. Those who are in complete denial and still waiting for total recovery, cannot even start to grieve.

Strategies for survival

There are a range of different ways of reacting to illness - which can be seen as forming a spectrum. At one end is denial of the illness, refusal to accept that there is a serious problem, or that the person needs to do anything about it. At the other end of the spectrum is over-acceptance of the illness, giving up any struggle, and descending into a life of invalidism. Somewhere in the middle are responses that are balanced, realistic, considered. Each point on the spectrum might have some advantages at particular times, and for particular people. The extreme positions are likely to lead to problems, but it is a mistake to be critical or judgmental about anyone's strategies for dealing with life.

Denial is the simplest of psychological strategies for coping with things that cannot be faced. It can at times be a useful mechanism, it will allow someone to carry on in a frightening or dangerous situation, not becoming upset by the immediate threat to life. It is a common response to finding evidence of illness in oneself. It can occur in cancer, with tragic results because delay reduces the chances of successful treatment. It can also occur in mental illness. It is a surprising fact that the average time that people with psychosis go before having treatment is one to two years. There are a number of factors explaining this, but denial is one of them. Denial has a place in coping with illness of any kind. It can allow people to focus on good options and keep hoping for the best. However it is only one strategy, and by itself makes for a limited response.

McGlashan (1987) has described two contrasting recovery styles following psychosis, 'sealing-over' and 'integration'. Sealing-over is like denial, involving minimising the significance of what is happening and not wanting to find out more about it. He suggests that the styles he described were fairly fixed aspects of people's personality.

I believe that the strategy of denial, and the style of sealing-over are linked to how people are treated. For a long time patients were encouraged to deny their symptoms. I was involved in a programme designed to make our service more responsive to people suffering from psychotic symptoms and as part of that we had to review how good we were at talking to our patients about their psychotic experiences. In an experienced and thoughtful team we found that we were not good at all. It is difficult and embarrassing to talk to people about their strange experiences. We found that as 'mental health professionals' we were adept at normalising things. People could say the most weird and alarming things and be greeted by a bland reassuring response. Patients were often subjected to probing questions about their 'mental state' when doctors wanted to make a diagnosis, but rarely offered the opportunity to talk openly about the unusual experiences that they were having. We had to learn about 'talking about psychosis', and then found it was useful, indeed essential if we wanted to help people. This was not therapy or some clever new approach, but simply something that too easily gets left out.

Denial as a basic approach is encouraged by medical advice which says that if only you do what you are told, if only you get the right treatment, take the right tablets, you will make a complete recovery. There is a fatal passivity in "being a good patient", which is the opposite of the attitude that is needed to overcome such a severe personal setback. Denial involves not looking at the emotional impact of what has happened, just hoping for the best in the face of adverse findings. It involves pretending you are O.K. when you are really nothing of the sort. The message is that the only good outcome is getting back to how you were before, and being able to forget the whole thing ever happened. It offers a solution which arises for a few, but which is not available for the great majority of people.

Reactions of the self to mental illness are important to understanding recovery. Without some outside support or action, reactions are likely to be overwhelmingly negative. The possibility of people developing an open and receptive attitude to their problems and to receiving help will depend on what they encounter. In this it is the attitudes of those they meet that are going to have a major influence. It is therefore a cause for concern that attitudes towards the mentally ill have been found to be as negative in the health service as anywhere else. Attitudes are conveyed by behaviour and manner more than by statements. In order to help people the attitude has to be strongly positive. It has to find ways to overcome the negative impression that people get from being treated as psychiatric patients. It is difficult not to convey the message that someone has done something wrong if you are taking away their freedom and keeping them in hospital. A concept of recovery that implies that failure to get better is the result of not being a good patient is not helpful.

The Attractions of Despair

There is another side to the story. Our society, so obsessed with success and appearances, is also drawn to images of damage and destruction. Literature, films, and music are full of stories of damaged and despairing people: people who have lost their way, given up, almost been left for dead in the struggle to the top. These are a common theme. Heroes tend to be people who are damaged in some way, and therefore at some distance outside the system.

What are the attractions of damage and despair? Why do people who are already feeling depressed about their lives like listening to songs about hopeless despairing people? This is not a minority interest. We are all drawn to these images, and narratives of lives that are similarly affected. People want stories about people like themselves or preferably people even worse off than themselves.

There is a curious mechanism whereby any reported account, once it is set down, acquires a certain credibility. There is comfort and hope in the recorded account. However bad things were, however much it cost the individual, the experience was survivable. What is more it was interesting and worthy of study. So reading accounts of people whose lives are even worse than our own is strangely comforting.

We identify with people going through something similar. It is possible to hear from another things one has not yet expressed oneself. This is a creative process, which helps the person gain a better understanding of his or her self. Often it seems people want this even more than they want to feel better. The strength of narrative accounts is that they communicate a meaningful sequence of events at a deep level. What has been random, malign, meaningless, can begin to fall into a pattern. The effect of accepting a story as being analogous to one's own can be quite dramatic. What is gained is a type of understanding which can help the person to recover a sense of purpose and hope. This can even happen if the story you identify with is apparently grim and hopeless.

There is also strength in numbers. The media repeatedly show us people loudly and fearlessly admitting their defeat by the world. There is a rejection of conventional values - exemplified by job, marriage or just adult responsibilities. This represents a celebration of giving up. It is a wilful going over to the other side. No more pushing on towards unachievable goals, no more putting up a façade of coping with the demands of society. And what a society!

There is a large group of people who think and say and write that today's society is all wrong. The "new age" movement, for example, includes many who see fitting in with western society as inevitably bad for your health. Instead of being "bent out of shape by society's pliers" people should be true to themselves. There is no need to prove anything to anyone - especially yourself. From this perspective the wounds gained from doing battle with the world are signs of honour, evidence of true intent. Despair with the world is justified because the world is wrong.

Images of alternative, gentler worlds have always been offered by poets and other dreamers. They have been enjoyed by a fairly limited audience of educated people. These people, who might enjoy harmless "escapist" literature, have generally led conventional lives, restricted by the pressures of society. People could enjoy the fantasy that life could be different, but knew that this was not really the case. What is new now is that the alternative culture is larger, more vocal, and due to the welfare state, better off. There is now a group of people who do not want to fit in with mainstream society, and can make an alternative life into a viable option.

So, despairing of life, or of the life that you have been trying to live, can have a great attraction. It is a radical option. It may be something that people savour as a fantasy to sustain them during very bad times. It can be a source of comfort, an antidote to feelings of complete powerlessness. For the majority life will go on more or less as it has been, but dark imaginings are a form of escape. Imagining alternative futures is a vital step on the way to being able to change your life. The well-known platitude about a crisis being an opportunity will only be true if alternatives are allowed to emerge. One of the big drawbacks of the medical recovery concept is that it is profoundly conservative. If the aim is to get back to normal, to how things were before, then dark thoughts have no place, and are part of the abnormality that needs to be suppressed. The need to adapt and seek a different future may be vital for recovery.

Adaptation or Denial

Ability to adapt to change may be the single most important characteristic in deciding how people cope with mental turmoil. Some people have a rigidity that makes any change very difficult. However it is wrong to see this simply as a trait of the individual. How flexible and open to change someone is will depend on many factors in their life. These will include their health, their financial security and their relationships.

The need to adapt is not part of the narrow medical concept of recovery. That view presents the disturbing experiences as abnormal and pathological. The person will get the message that what they have been experiencing is unreal or imaginary, something for which they need treatment, so that it will go away, and they will be themself again.

Lessons from voice hearers

The way that people react to hearing voices is an illustration of the differing strategies available to people. The traditional medical response says that the voices are not real; they are a part of a mental illness from which the person is suffering. The most common diagnosis given to someone who reports hearing voices is schizophrenia, although if they are very recent it might be described as an acute psychotic episode. The main medical intervention is antipsychotic medication. The advice is that if you take the medication then it should make the voices go away. There is no clear rationale for this; any more than there is an explanation of why paracetamol will help pain. It is just something that works, so you should take the advice, and medication that is offered.

When voices first occur they may be sudden, intrusive and very frightening. The medication may help the person to feel less anxious, and it may stop the voices completely. If that happens the crisis in the person's life may settle down, so that they are able to move on. For many people that strategy does not work. They are given a medical explanation of the voices, and they take the medication, but they continue to hear the voices. This gives the person the worst of both worlds. The voices are still perceived to be real, which casts doubt on everything said by the doctors. This may well be pointed out by the voices, whose message then undermines attempts at medical treatment. The medical message - that the voices are not real, and simply part of an illness - makes it difficult for the person to develop a better strategy for dealing with them.

Exciting new approaches to helping people who hear voices have been developing over the past fifteen years, starting with the work of the Dutch psychiatrist, Marius Romme. He started by getting together groups of people who hear voices, and looking at what strategies people had worked out for living with their voices. Romme and Escher found that the four strategies of:

- Distraction,
- Ignoring,
- Selective listening,
- Setting limits

were enough to characterise how people reacted to their voices.

Selective listening involves paying attention to positive voices and disregarding negative ones. Limit setting involves limiting the amount of time each day during which the person will pay attention to the voices. Less than half the group felt that they could cope with the voices. The copers were more likely to be using the strategies of selective listening and limit setting. The experience of hearing voices was described as falling into three stages

- The first "startling" phase was marked by anxiety and fear following the sudden onset of the voices
- The second "organisation" phase involved finding out how to cope with the voices, by trying out different strategies. Distraction and ignoring were rarely successful.
- The third "stabilisation" phase involved the voices becoming part of everyday life, with the person more in control again.

Before people can develop coping strategies it seems to be important for them to gain some understanding of the voices. They have to decide what the voices mean.

"Unless some meaning is attributed to the voices, it is very difficult to begin the phase of organising one's relationship with them in order to reduce anxiety" (Romme and Escher 1993).

It is stressed that people need explanations that they can accept. These tend to be normalising, presenting the voices as simply one form of human experience. The content of the voices then helps the person understand the origins of the experience by linking it to past loss or trauma or abuse.

Thomas in *"Dialectics of Schizophrenia"* (1997) has described his work in this area. He describes a dramatic case of a woman who had been troubled by voices, which had caused her to attempt to kill someone. She was able to regain control of her life by entering into a dialogue with the voices. Thomas stressed the vital importance of the meaning to the person of what the voices say. It is possible to help the person by getting them to clarify the message

- what is being said, who by, and why. Those are necessary preliminaries to developing a response to and a way of coping with the voices. However there is a conflict here with the usual medical approach usually begins with the non-negotiable statement that voices are caused by mental illness.

Those who hear voices usually come up with explanations which imply that the voices, or at least the messages are real. Thus they may think the voice is their dead mother comforting them, or their childhood abuser taunting them. This raises a real difficulty for doctors, since these supposedly helpful explanations will also be seen as symptoms of mental illness. This is a illustration of how it can be unhelpful to impose an explanation on the person whose life is being explained.

Caution

The recent work with people who hear voices is a tremendous advance. It began in a simple way with people being listened to and taken seriously. It quickly moved on to establish support groups for voice hearers, and there is now a Hearing Voices Network. This is a major social breakthrough, enabling an oppressed and denigrated minority to challenge the systems that have failed them. Understandably many of those involved are angry with the psychiatric system. The work described returns autonomy to the individuals. It is them developing an understanding of their voices that counts – one that they have found more helpful than the usual neuro-psychiatric explanation.

The caution concerns explanations, models and systems. They are inextricably linked to power. When people argue for their particular model against a rival, you witness a struggle for power. This is often apparent from the emotion that is generated. It is like a clash of religions, with each convinced that their version is the correct one. For them the long struggle is over because they have at last arrived at the truth. Power comes from being on the winning side, or on the side whose theories are in the ascendancy. The medical model was in power for a long time. There have been battles within that camp between psychotherapists and organic doctors who prescribe drugs, but now the drugs seem to be winning. Those opposing the medical model play the same game. They point out all the inconsistencies in psychiatry, and then come up with their own answer. So this is the model game; it has little to do with enlightening the world and a lot to do with professional competition.

All this warfare between different groups is somehow connected to trying to find measures to help people with mental illness. It is easy to lose sight of that point. Thomas (1997) describes the exciting developments in voice hearing, to which he has himself made a contribution. He does not conceal the very practical and down to earth origins of the work. It started with a patient being dissatisfied with the treatment she was getting for her auditory hallucinations, and was developed using information from other voice hearers about how they coped with their voices. He described at length a remarkable patient who he was able to help to gain control of her voices by talking to them. This work is very interesting, and may certainly help people. What is questionable is what Thomas did next. He went on to a bout of very rarefied philosophical theorising, bringing in the philosopher George Herbert Mead and the Russians Lev Vygotsky and Mikael Bakhtin. The production of his theory arose from the observations of the voice hearers. It follows the interesting finding that one of the difficulties for psychiatrists trying to help voice hearers is that the illness explanation is particularly unhelpful.

Each of the warring theories starts out in a limited field, where it is the framework of some existing intervention. The intervention is part of the core activity of the discipline that advances the model. It is probably a good intervention very effective within the area where it evolved. It may also be quite an impressive intervention, so that those who become involved become converts. There is then an expansionist phase, which can lead on to a bid to take over and colonise the whole field of mental health - and beyond. In this way the nugget of inspiration that is contained in the original observation, is stretched way beyond its useful field of application. What started out as a technique useful for certain people, ends up as a model to which people become emotionally, professionally and financially attached. It becomes a tyranny.

I am not accusing Thomas of imperialist tendencies. However it is worrying to see such a rapid move from some helpful techniques to a grand abstract theory. None of the techniques work with more than a percentage of those with troublesome symptoms. The enthusiastic description of single cases is interesting and inspiring, but should not lead to general theories.

My solution - to the problem of mental illness - is that there is and can be no general solution. There is no general theory that can inform our decisions.

There are lots of approaches and techniques, but they do not join up to make a grand scheme. This fact of life is constantly covered over by our fear of ignorance and uncertainty. Doctors and other would-be helpers need to have ready answers. There are also the market forces within the field that reward people for making claims and developing systems. My conclusion is that none of the theories is true, they are at best working hypotheses. In this respect mental health differs from other branches of medicine. In medicine there are scientific principles that have to be followed, whatever else is going on. If someone's blood sugar is very low they will die soon if it is not raised. If the pressure inside someone's skull remains too high they will not survive. If a baby is not delivered it will die. If infection is out of control the person may not survive. In these cases, action to put things right will depend on well-established principles of scientific medicine. The scope for individual choice is limited. Science has established basic principles that no doctor can ignore.

In psychiatry there are no such basic principles. At times doctors in psychiatry have claimed that there is a core of essential interventions, which must be prescribed by experts. Like the medical examples, these concern life and death issues. For example, some psychiatrists think that ECT is essential for people who are refusing food and drink because of their disturbed mental state. However this is never so clear-cut; even in extreme cases there will be a variety of options. If science can not provide the basic principles that a psychiatrist has to rely on in a crisis, then the only alternatives are ethical and legal ones. This is an important conclusion. The ultimate criteria in deciding what to do in a psychiatric emergency are ethical, not scientific.

A key issue is strategy. A person needs to have some way that they can regain the feeling that their problems are under control. With mental health there are always several different ways in which symptoms can be tackled. It is a question of what helps the person. If it helps to believe that the voice that bullies you night and day is your dead mother, then it helps. Psychiatry with its scientific pretensions has difficulty with this. It sometimes seems that in psychiatry being right has a higher priority than helping someone to get better. This is a profound problem. Doctors tend to have strong beliefs about the world, and people and science. They hold their theories as articles of faith. things that are thought or assumed to be true are not seen as beliefs but as facts of life.. That is why questioning them is not a matter for discussion and debate.

It is often said that there are similarities between psychiatrists and priests. Both deal in difficult, grey areas where certainty is lacking. Both have much knowledge and experience of their particular areas, for which people turn to them at times of trouble. Priests know about people's spiritual needs, their insecurity, their desire for more than just material survival. Psychiatrists know a lot about mental health, and how once it is lost, life can become unbearable. Yet both have one major drawback as sources of advice; they come with definite ideas about what the answers to people's problems will be. The idea of a partnership between professional and patient founders if the professional knows all the answers (or at least thinks he or she does). This would be swiftly denied by any psychiatrist, or psychologist – who will make much of patients making their own decisions. However the "mental health" viewpoint inevitably means that the individual's problems will be looked at from one particular angle.

Many professionals have a genuine desire to think laterally, and avoid imposing a narrow view of the world on people. However there has been a steady growth of government prescription of what is right for people. Professionals are employed and regulated by the government and are expected to implement policy. This means that in the cooperative partnership supposedly developing between professional and client there is a third party, telling both what to do.

Part II
The Reality of Personal
Survival and Recovery

Chapter 7
EVIDENCE OF RECOVERY

Where is the evidence that recovery from mental illness is possible? What does the evidence show? There are research studies, anecdotes, prejudices, and assumptions, but not much clarity. It will all depend what people mean by recovery, and how they set about investigating it.

What kind of "recovery"?

"Recovery", in this discussion is in danger of becoming meaningless. There are two fairly clear ways that people in the mental health field are using the term "recovery" –

1) Clinical recovery

This is the state of a subject, as assessed at a particular point in time, by another person; preferably a professional researcher. The assessment should be *objective*, which means it will involve looking for the presence of symptoms, and for evidence of "normal" function. It will be *statistical* – in that it will only be meaningful when compared with the results of other groups of people – either "normals", or people with a similar condition. Recovery assessed in this way may be "dimensional", where every person gets a score indicating the extent of their recovery, or "categorical", where people are judged as falling into a particular category such as 'recovered', or 'partly recovered', or 'not recovered', according to agreed criteria.

2) Personal recovery

This is the state of a person whose life has regained some meaning and purpose. It means that the person is able to get on with their life, and regain some dignity and self-respect. This is a more humanistic, non-professional way of looking at people. It is how people think about themselves. Recovery of this kind is a process on which all may be able to embark. Its progress will not be reflected in scores - using traditional tests of symptom rating scales. It is something to which people who go through periods of mental illness are now seen as Having a right.

Until recently this aspect of recovery was largely ignored in research on mental health problems. However, there are now many initiatives to collect and study people's thoughts and feelings about their lives and problems as they undergo recovery. User Focused Monitoring involves training people who have had experience of mental illness to interview people about their experiences of illness and treatment. This is being used increasingly as a sensitive way of assessing the value to individuals of services that are being provided.

These two different conceptions of recovery connect with each other in many ways, but are in conflict in others. For example, some degree of clinical improvement may be necessary before anyone is going to be able to rebuild their life and their self-esteem. However, the correlation between the different conceptions of recovery is not as close as doctors have assumed in the past – that treating people's symptoms was the way to guarantee their recovery. This fact is one of the major themes of this book.

History of recovery

Historical accounts show that the outlook for people suffering from mental illness has varied considerably over the centuries. The eighteenth century in England was depicted as a bad time when patients were neglected in the private madhouses. However more detailed research has shown that there were some good places, from which a large proportion of patients were discharged in a recovered condition (W.Parry-Jones, 1972). Then in the early nineteenth century moral treatment achieved discharge rates of up to 70% described as improved or recovered. (Beckoven J., 1972)

Joseph Conolly (1794-1866) was a pioneer of the non-restraint movement, when he was working at Hanwell Asylum, near London, in 1839. He abolished all restraint within four months of arriving at Hanwell, and then spent ten years improving the system. It is interesting that during this period of optimism and innovation recovery rates went up. This was not due to the introduction of any new treatment, but to the influence of an enlightened regime. Conolly was a strong advocate of the importance of non-specific factors in treatment. He was critical of claims made for specific treatments. He wrote, "*young and sanguine practitioners usually feel dissatisfied with candid statements of the possible inefficacy of medicines.*" He described how, during his lifetime, many powerful treatments had been abandoned. These included large bloodletting, violent purges and the excessive employment of mercury. He put down the lack of specific therapeutic agents to the "extreme obscurity of the causes of insanity". He said that people should not be ashamed of lack of knowledge. The people who had day to day contact with the patients, the attendants, were the most important part of his system. He said that the physician needs cheerful, healthy helpers, of natural good disposition and possessed of good sense. He should seek to preserve their cheerfulness, health and contentment. "*They are his instruments and he should keep them finely tempered*" (Conolly1856; quoted by Leigh D. 1961). Unfortunately the optimistic mood did not last. As the asylums became more overcrowded, so the chances of people recovering went down.

Follow-up studies

Kraepelin is a key figure in the history of how people recover. He became a professor of psychiatry in Germany, and produced nine editions of his influential textbook between 1883 and 1926. He put forward the idea that if you could identify groups of patients with similar symptoms, then you were likely to find that they had the same brain pathology and the same things causing it. He developed a way of classifying patients which has lasted to the present day. He identified one group which he called "Dementia praecox" (literally means senility of the young), which corresponds roughly to what was later called schizophrenia. He reported that 80% of people with this condition showed steady deterioration. It was a fairly hopeless condition. His view was very influential, and corresponds to one of the stereotypes of the mentally ill which has persisted to this day: that the condition shows a progressive downhill course, and does not respond to anything you can do. This is about as negative as you can be. Coupled to this is the idea that the illness is due to some kind of brain disease that has probably been inherited.

This was the starting point at the beginning of the twentieth century, against which all later investigators have been reacting. The studies are difficult to interpret because different writers have used different definitions of mental illness and of recovery. However the consistent finding is that things are not nearly as bleak as Kraepelin said. It is also notable that, one hundred years later, the causes and brain pathology have never been identified.

Manfred Bleuler (1974) did a 20 year follow-up of 208 patients who had been admitted to the Burghlozli Clinic in Zurich, Switzerland. He found complete remission in 20% and good improvement in another 20%. Only 24% were still severely disturbed. He found that good outcomes were less common once the person had been ill for over five years. Bleuler concluded that:

> "Generations of psychiatrists felt that schizophrenia was a process psychosis, progressing to complete deterioration, if life was long enough to allow the process to come to an end. I am certain today that the contrary is true."

Bleuler had literally grown up with schizophrenia since it was his father Eugen Bleuler who first developed the concept. His father was director of the Burghlozli Clinic, so the son was acquainted with people suffering from schizophrenia from his childhood onwards. In his study he describes how many of his chronic patients improved later in life, rather than deteriorating.

Ciompi (1980) was based in Lausanne, Switzerland, and followed up 300 patients after 37 years. He found that 49% had a good outcome.

Prof. G Harrison et al (2001) reported on the 15 and 25 year follow-up of the International Study of Schizophrenia. This is a modern study using carefully standardised ways of assessing people. It was a collaboration between workers at 18 sites around the world. Over 50% were rated as having favourable outcomes, and had not had a psychotic episode for the past two years. The conclusion of the International Study of Schizophrenia was:

"Schizophrenia and related psychoses are best seen as episodic disorders with a rather favourable outcome for a significant proportion of patients. Because expectations can be so powerful a factor in recovery, patients families and clinicians need to hear this."

Economic perspective

Warner (2004) has claimed that the percentage of people who recover is affected by the economic conditions present in society. As an example of this he said that the recovery rate was halved during the depression of the 1920's and '30's. This was part of a larger thesis in which Warner applied what he called a materialist approach, stating that:

" ... in order to understand human thought and behaviour it is essential to begin with the material conditions of mankind's existence and productive processes."

He concluded that:

"Recovery rates from schizophrenia were not significantly better at the end of the twentieth century than they were at the beginning."

If schizophrenia has had a different outcome at different periods of history, this would help to explain why researchers have come to such varied conclusions. According to Warner, Kraepelin's patients were mostly admitted to hospital during the great depression of the late nineteenth century. It was a time of high unemployment, when mental institutions were overcrowded and their regimes barren and coercive. This will have contributed to the pessimistic prognosis that Kraepelin thought was inevitable in schizophrenia.

One of the consistent findings from follow-up studies is that clinical recovery - loss of symptoms - and social recovery, - ability to function in society -, do not go together. It is commonly found that persisting symptoms are not a barrier to social function. Mason et al (1995) who carried out the Nottingham 13 year follow-up study say:

"the status of symptoms may have little relevance to everyday social functioning."

International perspective

The World Health Organisation has done a lot of work comparing the outcomes of schizophrenia in different countries. There appears to be a consistent finding that outcomes are better in poorer countries. In one major study from the 1970's it was found that, at five years, twice as many people were free of symptoms in poorer countries (Leff et al 1992). Many different theories can be advanced to explain such findings. However, at the very least they must raise questions about whether the specific drug treatments, which are much more widely used in the richer countries, do anything to improve outcome in the long run.

The situation of people suffering from psychosis is very different in different cultures. The social pressures that make recovery difficult for people in the UK are not things that can be easily overcome. Lack of a supportive extended family, poor housing, stigmatisation, inactivity and social isolation all affect chances of recovery. Low stress environments are difficult to find here, which goes some way to explain why fairly few people manage to recover without help from medication. It is a mistake to conclude from cross-cultural studies that 'recovery without medication' is an option that psychiatrists in the west simply ignore. It may be a more realistic option in cultures where it is genuinely possible for people who are recovering to adapt their life-style to their needs.

Personal clinical experience

I have known many people who were suffering from schizophrenia, some for over twenty years, and what I have seen fits in with Bleuler's view. Rather than steadily deteriorating, people with schizophrenia tend to improve. They improve provided they are not stressed and disturbed to the extent that they suffer from relapses. That is a very big proviso, because the living-conditions in the UK for people who are trying to recover following schizophrenia have been difficult and harsh. If they suffer a relapse, there is a return of acute symptoms and the person's life is interrupted. They may then behave in ways that threaten their social position and jeopardise their future. They may lose jobs, relationships and accommodation. "Relapse" is really an oversimplification of what happens. It covers a range of ways that a person's mental health may deteriorate, usually under the influence of some kind of stress. Being drawn back into the mental health system, maybe as an involuntary patient, can add greatly to the life disruption that occurs; yet at times it is unavoidable.

Most of the old studies of schizophrenia were carried out at a time when the approved treatment for the condition was admission to a mental hospital. Once there the person would lose contact with the outside world, and stay in for years on end. There were some benevolent people working in the hospitals, but the remoteness of the hospitals from normal life is difficult now to appreciate. The quality of life for patients was very poor, so that the fact that some people came out of that system and went on with their lives is testament to the human spirit.

The mental hospitals finally went out of favour during the 1970s and 80s, and the closure programme quickly gathered pace. This was done at a time when 'Naïve Psychiatry' was very much the official line. It seems genuinely to have been believed that discharging people, and then closing the hospitals would actually solve the problems (and even save money.) This led to a period during which care for people suffering from schizophrenia became, if anything, even worse than before. Instead of being confined in hospital, people had short periods in hospital followed by hasty discharge. There was little support available, and a naïve belief that once out of hospital everything would be all right. For some this worked, but for the majority it did not. One consequence was the start of "revolving door" patients, people who were discharged out through the door, only to be readmitted again quite soon. They suffered frequent relapses, each leading to another short admission. Their symptoms would be brought under control with drugs, and they would then be discharged back to the same bad conditions as before. Many of the revolving door patients ended up by killing themselves; a few harmed other people. They could see that there was no way out of the depressing cycle that they had got onto. Others survived, and eventually managed to live without the frequent crisis admissions. Some managed to form useful links with people in the hospitals - both staff and patients - so that they established support systems for themselves.   One point that comes out of this is that follow-up studies of groups of patients will reflect what was going on at the time. All they can tell you is how a particular generation of patients got on with the conditions that they faced. The conditions include: available treatments, support outside hospital, attitudes in the community, and levels of wealth and employment in society.

There are now new services such as assertive out-reach and home treatment with the specific aim of improving the position of people recovering from mental illness. There are great hopes that services are at last being developed which will end the days of "revolving door patients." Social support in the form of housing and finance are also better now than they were twenty years ago. However it will be another 10 or 20 years before the long-term effects of the new arrangements can be assessed. Policy making always has to move beyond firm evidence to correct problems that may have been created a generation earlier.

The "revolving door" problem followed from the idea that achieving remission of symptoms by medical treatment is the same as achieving recovery. What can be achieved in an acute psychiatric unit will always be quite limited. Acute treatment aims to get people's symptoms and behaviour under control. Such units are extremely costly in financial, psychological and spiritual terms. A large proportion of the money spent on psychiatry still goes on acute treatment - the goal of which is to get people back to how they were before the latest crisis. Being a patient on an acute ward will not by itself equip someone to cope better with his or her life. It is not helpful to talk about a "natural history" of schizophrenia. This idea was favoured at a time when people with a diagnosis of schizophrenia were the most alienated and marginalised group in society. The so-called natural history reflected people coping with that predicament. Recovery factors have to be present in people's environment for them to be able to take advantage of them. Schizophrenia may have a better long-term outcome than its name and its popular image suggests. One important finding is that the outcome is very variable – and so very difficult to predict. This means that in any individual case the outcome may be good. The diagnosis is thus not a good predictor of how recovery will go, (another reason to question the usefulness of the diagnostic process.)

People diagnosed with a bipolar disorder have by contrast traditionally been seen as having a good prognosis. They have been hailed as triumphs of psychiatric treatment. This is because their symptoms often go completely while the are undergoing periods of intensive treatment in hospital. Anthony, described in chapter 1, is an example of this. He seemed to do very well, but had continuing problems, and that seems to be a common finding. The short term responsiveness of the condition made people conclude that recovery was easily achieved. Long term studies have not supported this. Anthony showed some of the problems that can follow from having a condition that doctors mistakenly believe is easy to treat. This has allowed excessive reliance on medical treatment to continue.

Prognosis –science or guesswork?

Giving a prognosis, or prediction of how someone's condition will affect them in the future has always been a part of the medical mystique. Doctors were expected to finish their assessment with a definite statement of prognosis. They could build a reputation being good prognosticians. This is a particularly dubious part of psychiatry. Making a prognosis in cases of the "major mental illnesses" (such as schizophrenia) depended on detailed attention to the minutiae of the abnormal mental experiences. The theory was that these would reveal the nature of the underlying illness. It was an obscure and mysterious art – calling for years of experience and familiarity with a large literature base. The problem was that a prognosis given with such authority and acted upon could easily alter the course of someone's life.

The question therefore becomes really important - whether giving prognoses is backed up by any good evidence; or misguided and potentially harmful? The extent to which people are affected by expectations is greater in mental health than in most other branches of medicine. Patients struggle against prejudice and negative stereotypes, and yet psychiatry itself has been a major source of these. Telling someone that they have a bad prognosis may be harmful – but so may a failure to advise someone about the seriousness of the problems. However, these two are very different. One may need to be very frank and open in helping someone come to terms with how serious their problems have become. Talking realistically and honestly about the present may be difficult and painful, but in the end helpful. This is nothing like making soothsayer-like predictions about how someone's life is going to turn out. That exercise is harmful and cannot claim any scientific justification.

For a long time, and to some extent even now, people refer to being in hospital for a prolonged period, as a base line against which they measure the success of interventions. "In the past he would have spent months (or years) in hospital", is used to justify the poor state of what may be offered. I have come across some workers who have never been near a long stay hospital using the same kind of argument. The opposite case is also made, in which "the old asylum" is idealised. If only there were such places now, it is argued, they would be just what we need. In reality, prolonged periods in institutions were found to have many adverse effects. What they also did was cut people off from most naturalistic recovery factors. This may have strengthened the idea that the condition that the person suffered from had a "natural history".

Thus, to summarise: medical studies show that a significant proportion of people (up to about 50%), diagnosed as suffering from major psychiatric illness, will lose most symptoms and be able to live normal lives. Those who have continuing symptoms or recurrent episodes are likely to find that their lives will be different because of their mental health problem, and adaptation and change will be needed to live with the problems. These can be seen as part of the recovery process, rather than as evidence of failure to recover. The presence of symptoms does not rule out a return to a rewarding and valuable way of life. However to achieve this will depend on the resources and options available, not on the imagined course of an illness.

Positive and negative conceptions of recovery

The studies mentioned above all used a concept of clinical recovery. They measured symptoms and assessed function. These are the traditional objective ways of looking for recovery. They are negative, in that improvement involves a decrease in scores. They do not say very much about the experience and achievements of the individuals.

There is a negative bias that runs all through psychiatry. When someone goes to see a psychiatrist, the first thing that happens is that a "psychiatric history" is taken. This involves a thorough review of all the problems that have occurred in a person's life. It starts by asking whether there has been any mental illness in the family. Then there is the pregnancy and delivery, where any physical complications are sought. Then there is childhood. Here there are any number of physical, psychological or social setbacks that can be encountered. This process goes on right up to the present day. Once the history has been compiled, which may take several hours; a formulation is constructed, gathering together all the significant findings. The findings are all to do with pathology, things that are wrong. There will usually be enough material to support a wide range of theories about why the person has had a mental breakdown, and why their prognosis may doubtful. Background factors are uncovered that have made the person vulnerable to mental instability. The problem is that there is too much evidence, and there are no ways of deciding how significant or abnormal any particular item is. The lives of people who have no psychiatric problems might contain similar items. There is much scope for the bias and cultural expectations of the psychiatrist to influence how he or she interprets this information.

The vulnerability factors identified in the history are in the past - and so not amenable to change. Even if a person's present symptoms improve, they will still be seen as someone with serious problems. They are so vulnerable that any apparent normality is seen as a superficial veneer. It can result in a psychiatrist being suspicious or even critical of an apparent improvement. It is said to be only superficial, because the underlying problems "have not been dealt with". This is the sort of thinking that supports negative expectations.

The problem of a detailed psychiatric assessment is that it portrays an individual as someone who doesn't have a chance. It becomes surprising that the person has lasted as long as they did. It provides material that can be used to support all sorts of theories about why the person has problems. Most of these theories are speculative and unprovable, but they help to build a negative story, and undermine a positive forward-looking approach.

One way to avoid this negative bias is to make the history focus on strengths as well as weaknesses. This is good in theory, but in practice strengths tend to be less conspicuous than weaknesses. If you assess someone in their thirties who is having major mental health problems for the first time, then you will know that they possess most of the skills needed to get by in life. You know that after this time of trouble, they should be able to move on in their life. The trouble is that they do not know this. They may well have reached the point where they are convinced that they will never be able to carry on. At times of crisis the person's negative thoughts will be loud and insistent. It will be difficult to elicit strengths from such a person, and easy to get a long list of deficiencies. The rehearsal of all the problems that the person has encountered in their life can have a negative effect.

There is a further disadvantage to the historical approach. It tends to present the person as so damaged and disadvantaged that it opens up a wide gap between doctor and patient. The display of a lifetime of problems, can lead to the incorrect conclusion that the person is a hopeless case and is suffering from a personality disorder. This in turn may prejudice people against trying to help the person.

There is a whole literature that looks at people's lives in a more positive way. There are many personal accounts of people who have survived mental illness. These describe how people have overcome difficulties and apparent vulnerabilities to regain control of their lives.(Lovejoy, 1984; Deegan, 1996; Leete, 1989; Coleman, 1999.) These may be helpful for people who are experiencing similar problems and also for workers in the field who have no such experience.

There is also a growing literature looking not at illness and suffering, but at health and happiness. Michael Argyle (2001) was a social psychologist who made several contributions to improving mental health. His early work on non-verbal communication helped the development of social skills training. This aims to help people whose relationships and self-esteem suffer because they are bad at such things as non-verbal communication, rewardingness, understanding of others, and making conversation. This approach seems rather naïve to people with an analytical, psychiatric way of looking at things, but it has been found to be very helpful for those with problems in this area – such as people with Asperger's Syndrome. This is an example of helping people with what their actual problem is, rather than classifying and analysing them. Argyle went on to study happiness, and how people achieve it. Positive psychology is a growing area whose aim is "understanding and facilitating happiness and subjective well-being" (Carr A.2004). It is beginning to influence clinical psychology, but so far has had limited impact on how we think about mental illness. This is an area of study that is very relevant to recovery.

Positive conclusion

"Professionals need to believe that recovery is possible."
Having hope, being positive, valuing every small step that is made; these are some things that are essential to help people to recover. There is plenty in the "science" to support this, yet up to now experts have tended to interpret it in a particularly gloomy way. Anyone in this field who goes around spreading pessimism is doing more harm than good, and there is no justification for mental health services that undermine and underestimate potential. If services can't help people to recover, what is the point of them?

Chapter 8
THE LONG ROAD TO RECOVERY

The possibility that there is more to recovery than is contained in psychiatry was proved to me dramatically by a group of patients who I treated in the mid 1980s (Sankey A.,Hopkins I, & Whitwell D). This was early in my career as a psychiatrist, and these patients humbled me and brought home the limits of what I could do for people. This was a generation ago, an age in psychiatry, but the lessons have stayed with me, and I think they are still important. They were sixteen widows, all admitted to a psychiatric hospital suffering from severe psychiatric problems, including becoming depressed, suicidal and unable to cope on their own. Several were admitted to hospital after repeated suicide attempts. Only three of them had suffered from psychiatric problems before their bereavement. For the rest their depressed states appeared to be a gross accentuation of normal grieving. They almost all hated being in hospital, and most continued to say that they wished they had been allowed to die.

This group did not do well in hospital. It was not seen as a good place for them to be, but there was no alternative. At that time community services were poorly developed. It is a sign of how things have moved on that today it would probably be possible to help many of them without admitting them to hospital. Almost all had repeated admissions, having to be re-admitted because of getting worse after discharge. Suicide and severe self-neglect were seen as real risks. Many had total lengths of stay of over one year. The medical measures used to treat depression did not produce much improvement. Generally the admissions were long and unhappy. To the staff they seemed fairly fruitless - with little benefit to show apart from keeping the women alive. As we got to know the women, common background factors emerged. Many had had close, exclusive and dependent relationships with their husbands. Some described wonderful marriages, others unhappy battlegrounds.

The better we knew the individuals the more understandable their complete collapses became. This did not always help the staff to develop positive and sympathetic relationships with them. The role of long standing personality traits in contributing to the problems could make the staff feel that the person had always been like this, or that they were using their helplessness to manipulate people. This was an example of the way that detailed psychiatric assessment can confirm a negative impression.

Discharging the women from hospital was difficult, as they tended to become dependent on the ward, in spite of their continuing dislike of being there. We were able to offer some support at home but this was not enough for some who had to go into supported accommodation. As well as medical treatment and general support, about half the women were offered grief therapy with a psychologist. This involved facing and working with their grief in a systematic way. It was a new approach at that time, an early form of cognitive-therapy. An enthusiastic senior psychologist carried out this therapy, but it seemed to make very little difference to any of the women.

After seeing women with these problems over a number of years I was at a loss to know how to help them. In order to gain a better understanding I organised a follow-up study to see what had happened to them after they finally left us. At the time of discharge none had seemed anywhere near to recovery. The criteria of good outcome that we applied for the follow-up were ones established by Parkes & Weiss (1983). These were:

1) Return of feelings of well-being
2) Regained capacity to cope with the problems of everyday life
3) Decline in preoccupation with grief.

The women were seen again between one and four years after discharge by two of my colleagues, Alison Sankey and Ian Hopkins. This was not a research study, more an audit into an aspect of our service that was causing concern. The most striking finding was that by the time that they were seen, half the women were in the good outcome group. In other words half of these severely depressed and despairing women, who had seemed quite unable to manage their lives were now happy again. In each case the recovery seemed to be linked to new events, people and activities. In hospital, we, like the women had been overshadowed by the past. We had seen their past histories as making their stuckness all too understandable. The psychological help that was offered was also at that time largely focused on the past. It dealt much more with going over the disturbing memories of the bereavement, rather than looking to the future. The new events that subsequently helped them were nothing at all to do with treatment. They included getting involved in running a family business, getting part-time work and moving to be near a sister, and forming a new close relationship.

At follow-up some of the widows continued to suffer from depression, and lead very limited and unhappy lives. The most adverse outcome was a woman in her fifties who, as well as taking a number of overdoses, had also been having binges of heavy drinking. She suffered from depression and a paranoid state in which she felt frightened and unsafe when alone. A brain scan showed mild changes, which were considered to be compatible with early dementia. She showed no improvement in hospital and was eventually moved to a nursing home. I forgot about this woman until I met her again ten years later; long after our follow-up study was finished and had assigned her to the poor outcome group. She was still at the nursing home, but was planning to move to a flat of her own. It was a very homely nursing home, with mixed clientele and an owner who lived there with his wife and children. (It was probably not the sort of place that would be approved by today's standards.) My patient had settled down and made her home there, and had befriended the other residents including a woman with Down's syndrome. She had regained confidence and begun to attend a number of social groups in the town. The reason that she had come to see me was that she was wondering about moving out of the home into a flat of her own. Her memory had improved and she showed no signs of dementia. I was so surprised by her recovery that I asked a radiologist to look again at her brain scan. He said that it was true that it was compatible with dementia, but it was also compatible with normality. Such tests are notoriously difficult to interpret. The outcome of this little study was very humbling to a psychiatrist. It appeared that whereas psychiatry failed to assist recovery in this group (probably the reverse), once the patients got away from psychiatry they came across a range of curative factors in the outside world, which produced impressive improvements. These "naturalistic" factors are many and varied. They are alike in being unpredictable, and in being the result of initiatives of the person them self. Not only do professionals play down these factors, but it may be also that involvement with specialist services will cut people off from these health-giving influences.

Looking back I can see that the women were probably not ready to recover. We were trying to get them to move on, but they didn't want to. At times there seemed to be a battle of wills, and we felt we were losing. We had set ourselves the wrong goals. If we had had much more limited objectives we could have reached them, and the outcome might have been seen as good. After all, against considerable odds we did keep the women alive, we provided first aid. However because of the illness-treatment-recovery model that we were operating under, "just" keeping people alive through a crisis was not seen as the right thing to be doing.

Chapter 9
NATURALISTIC FACTORS IN RECOVERY

Many factors are thought to help recovery, but it is impossible to be sure which one has been important for any particular person. People try many different things, and then at last they recover, but they cannot tell what was decisive. My approach is not to try to introduce a system of factors; so the order in which they will be discussed is arbitrary. Naturalistic factors are those that occur without the involvement of any special mental health provision. They may be responsible for those cases of recovery that professionals regard as "spontaneous" or as due to "placebo effects". My thesis is that these should not be seen as minor peripheral phenomena, only of interest because they interfere with research into treatment. Rather they are the bedrock of how people recover, and in population terms more important than specific treatments.

1) Time

Time is an important factor, though for some reason most experts deny this. These are frequent questions: "How long will it take?" "When can I expect things to begin to improve?" Unfortunately it takes a long time to recover - it often seems far too long. When someone is distressed time may seem to go very slowly. It is difficult to get through the long days, when old interests no longer give pleasure. Going to bed may be the only thing to look forward to, with sleep the only release. For others the bed to which sleep does not come becomes a scene of further torment. Boredom can be a result of the slowing down of time with nothing to fill it.

There are many suggestions that the sort of major change involved in recovering from mental illness takes between eighteen months and three years. This period crops up repeatedly in different settings. It is a long time for anyone, and that may be part of its significance. It is long enough for forgetting, for moving on from how you have been. It is beyond the "attention span" of day-to-day life. At the end of such a time the train of thought is lost. It is so long that if you were waiting for something you will have given up. This can allow something else to happen. Time passing allows distractions, involvements, and new experiences to occur. Boredom can even be a stimulus.

Intense experience may lose its ability to startle after a time. This is seen with the sudden onset of hearing voices. In the early stages the person is in no state to work out any sort of strategy. The same is seen with panic attacks. At first they are overwhelming - making normal functioning very difficult. With time there may come more familiarity, and then strategies for survival can be worked out.

What is desperately wanted at the start is some immediate relief, an answer or solution. It is felt to be essential to get some improvement. To achieve this people may adopt drastic courses of action, such as stopping going out at all, knocking themselves out with drugs or alcohol, or committing suicide. To come in then and say that recovery takes a very long time may be very unhelpful. To someone who is suffering and finding it difficult to carry on, the idea of another month may be too much, let alone another year. To give such an opinion could prove fatal. A more useful question is 'what can be done to help?' The answer might be that psychiatry can offer a number of ways of alleviating symptoms and reducing distress. People are seen when in the midst of a crisis, and are offered short-term help. The pressure to do this is the highest priority in acute psychiatry. The trouble is that short-term measures tend to produce only temporary relief. Vigorous medical treatments - intensive support, medication, time off work, may produce a respite, but it is difficult to get round the eighteen month rule. The tendency to relapse will go on until a reasonable period of time has passed. In that period of time the mental health problems may come to seem endless. Much of the frantic activity that takes place in psychiatric units is providing first aid to get people through the next few weeks. If a broader concept of recovery is lacking, then the importance of the medium term time frame will be lost. In every acute episode, no matter how urgent the action that is needed straight away, the eighteen month plan needs to be developed. When this is done the central role of the individual and their life plans will be kept in focus. Often a vital role for psychiatry is to hold and support people who are not ready to recover.

Janice

Janice was a woman who had repeated crises with despair and attempts at suicide. She was in and out of hospital several times, with little real improvement. Her relationship had ended and she was lonely and despairing. She began to drink heavily, and would make desperate phone calls to the hospital when drunk. She had lost her job and was in danger of having nowhere to live. By this time she was becoming unpopular with the psychiatric team. When she was discussed there was emphasis on her drinking problem, and her long-standing difficulties in relationships. It began to be seen that she was not taking steps to help herself, but was using threats of suicide to manipulate people. It was felt that it was up to her if she chose to go on drinking, but that she should not be repeatedly bailed out by psychiatric services.

She had reached a state that Prof. Gethin Morgan(1991) has described as "malignant alienation". She was being seen as beyond help because she was bringing trouble on herself by her own actions. Then she successfully committed suicide.

I had the job of writing a summary of what had happened for the coroner. This was a painful process, which involved reviewing all that had happened, but now in a mood of sadness and guilt, rather than the irritation that she had generated in life. What struck me most strongly was that this whole saga had been played out in less than two years. At the start she had been working, in a relationship, with nothing to mark her down as a future suicide. The progressive slide downhill had knocked away all her supports, and she had become alienated from the system that was supposed to help her. Two years in these circumstances was a very long time for her to live through, but not long enough for her to recover. I cannot see any reason why she should not have recovered, except that she and those around her gave up. They did not consider the importance of time.

Psychiatric interventions tend to allow very little time. Drug treatments are expected to remove symptoms within days or weeks, after which the person is expected to be all right. A few weeks in hospital is regarded as satisfactory treatment for suicidal depression. The reality of how people change means that it is not practical, or desirable to stay in hospital until recovered. Hospital treatment is for acute symptoms, for certain limited medical interventions. This means that early "relapse" is very common. It is not really relapse at all but rather a sign that the time of mental distress that the person is passing through has not yet passed. These bad times often coincide with major life change, which themselves take a long time – interestingly, eighteen months to three years - to settle down. The bereavement study brought home the slowness with which people recover from major loss. It also showed how having unrealistic expectations of rapid change can lead to despair and alienation.

This is a real problem for those trying to offer help. The illness model leads people to conclude that if someone has not recovered in the allotted (fairly short) time, then they are not suffering from mental illness, but a personality disorder. This re-classification can have a very negative effect on both expectations, and attitudes to the person. One way to avoid the pitfalls of unrealistic expectations is to see periods of psychiatric treatment for what they are - periods of intensive support to get over certain particular problems, to get through a particular phase. They will not themselves bring about recovery, but should be seen as first aid; a form of crisis management.

Bereavement may be a case in which time is especially important. Grieving can dominate a person to such an extent that others have to step in to maintain life. The bereaved person can appear caught up in endless, self-destructive ruminations. Yet it does run its course, and people do reach a stage when they can move on. The ruminations and distress may serve purposes, provided they do not endanger life.

2) Relationships

For many people relationships are the key to their recovery. This would be regarded as obvious by many, but is treated with some scepticism by workers in the field. Psychiatry has tended to focus on the problems caused by relationships, rather than their benefits. In the past there was much talk about relationships, particularly those in the family, being a cause of mental illness. Such theories have fallen from favour even though there is much solid evidence that family relationships can affect the course of mental illness.

A series of studies were carried out at the Institute of Psychiatry in London from 1958 onwards looking at the impact of family relationships on relapse rates for schizophrenia and depression. It was found that people returning from hospital to live with close relatives were more likely to relapse than people living in hostels. Further work showed that relapses were more likely in those who were living with family members who showed features called 'Emotional over-involvement', 'Critical comments' or 'Hostility' (together referred to as Expressed Emotion or EE) when interviewed. Many different studies were carried out, the results being summarised by Bebbington and Kuipers in 1994. The results show that the findings are very consistent, with overall relapse rate in the first year being 54% in 'High EE' families, and 22% in 'Low EE' families. "EE" is an expression which unfortunately gets used in a pejorative sense, being critical of the family without any understanding of the complexity of the factors that result in this finding.

The EE story began as a study into factors leading to relapse, but quickly led to attempts to improve things. One way to interpret the results is to see them as showing that relationships are critical for people's well-being, that is, ordinary, non-professional relationships. The work was done in the 60's,70's and 80's, which were the era when naïve psychiatry was discharging patients home with limited continuing care. The finding that linked critical or over-involved families with high relapse rates was difficult to accept for families struggling very much on their own with a difficult situation. They lacked information, advice and practical help in dealing with their relative. They were also likely to be having trouble coming to terms with the changed fortunes of their relative; so they were grieving. Building on the EE findings, various ways were developed of trying to help families in this situation (Leff et al 1982). These involved meeting with the family and the patient, often on a regular basis over many months. The sessions would cover issues such as information sharing, communication skills training, and problem solving. These approaches moved beyond the negative message that something was wrong with the family, to seeing the family as the most potent agent available to help the patient. Results of this approach were good. A review of 25 clinical studies (Pritschel 2001) concluded that there was a 20% reduction in relapses in people whose families took part.

This example brings up the old question of whether the benefits are due to the particular style of help offered, or due to non specific effects. If one thinks back to the plight of the families, it is easy to see what an impact is made by regular meetings, support, problem solving etc. In the early 80's there were still debates about whether it was going to be cheaper to treat patients at home than keep them in poorly staffed long-stay hospitals. Money was very short and one of the few ways that people could get good support at home was by agreeing to become the subject of one of the family intervention pilot studies. I was involved with one of these projects and saw how amazed and pleased the families were to see us. For a time the family had a good level of support. However the fact that this was a treatment meant that after a time it stopped. The treatment model proposed that a short course of treatment would lead to changes in the family, leading to them being able to manage better in the future. This has been shown to work, although the benefits fall away with time. The family work does not remove the need for continuing access to a good level of support.

Those who work with people experiencing acute mental health problems can form a jaundiced view of relationships. In the past this found expression in the restrictions placed on patients in hospital from forming close relationships. Staff would actively discourage such relationships, and if patients found ways round the opposition, stronger measures would be taken. This would include discharging someone from hospital, and banning him or her from continuing to visit their friend/ would-be partner.

There are times when people who are mentally disordered need to be protected from rash behaviour - including the forming of new relationships. The most obvious case is where people suffer from mania and hypomania. In elevated mood states there is a rise in sexual interest and desire, and a fall in normal inhibitions. This can lead to consequences that are disastrous for the individual and their family. There are also times when people with psychotic symptoms seek to form relationships which are based on a misinterpretation of the situation. These are exceptional situations, in which mental health law allows professionals to step in and restrict the freedom of the individual. However it is the existence of these exceptional cases that has fostered an atmosphere in which the freedom of individuals to form relationships has been restricted. It has allowed the persistence of a culture in which professionals disapprove of patients forming new relationships with each other, even if this is not actually forbidden by law. Over the years I have known many couples who have met in hospital and have gone on to enjoy lasting loving relationships, important for their recovery.

If good relationships can help recovery, bad ones may prevent it. Among the events that can contribute to recovery are the endings of relationships. Divorce, separation and bereavement - which are such powerful causes of mental suffering, can also contribute. These facts support the idea that outside help to improve a relationship could help the recovery process.

Forming new relationships can offer hope for people who are struggling to recover but of course it may all go wrong; that is a risk that anyone faces. Avoiding all risk is a strategy that some people follow, but at great cost to themselves in the long run. It is a strategy that often seems to be implicit in the advice of professionals.

3) Life events and changes

The question of whether unpleasant experiences can lead to mental illness has a long and interesting history. There are many historical and fictional accounts of people being driven mad by the terrible things that have happened to them. It fits in with popular ideas, and the experiences that ordinary people have. Yet in the past psychiatrists have played down the possibility of events having such direct effects on people. This was due partly to the power of the concept of mental illness as something within the person, related to their biological make-up. It was said that mental illness was not caused by outside stress; the most that could be said was that an episode of illness was precipitated by stress.

The controversy over the significance of sexual abuse as a cause of mental disturbance is another example of how difficult psychiatrists have found it to accept that adverse life events can play a part in causing continuing mental health problems. Early in his career, Freud put forward the idea that the sexual abuse of children was the root cause of neurosis. However he moved away from that position to the more complicated but socially acceptable one that neurosis is caused by repressed fantasies of a sexual nature. This shift of emphasis from real to fantasy led to a corresponding diversion of the attention of therapists from the real world to the internal one. The preference for focusing on the contents of people's minds rather than their lives in the world has persisted.

We have been rescued, to some extent, from this obscure way of looking at the world by painstaking researches such as those of Prof. George Brown and his team. Prof. Brown is a sociologist who for forty years has carried out research into the way that events and social conditions affect people, and can bring about psychiatric disorder. He developed the semi-structured interview into a reliable way of getting accounts of personal experience that were free from observer bias. The question of how people are affected by outside events turned out to be very difficult to answer, because of the human tendency to look for explanations whenever anything goes wrong. If people were interviewed after some bad thing had happened to them, they would point to a wide range of events which might have caused the trouble. This happened even with occurrences such as having a Downs Syndrome baby, which could not have been caused by the event. The other problem is that many of the events that are offered as explanations may in fact be caused by the early stages of the mental disturbance that they are supposed to explain. Thus the loss of a job may be used to explain depression, but might have been caused by it.

Brown was the first to find reliable ways to identify events that affect people separately from any psychological effects that they may have produced. This careful work has confirmed what common sense had always assumed - that people are affected by their experiences. He has done much work on understanding the causes of depression, particularly in women. He found that adverse life events of the kind that have long term negative implications for the individual are common causes of depression. He also showed that having three young children to look after, having lost a parent in childhood, and having on-going life difficulties increase vulnerability to depression, whereas having a close confiding relationship was a protective factor.

This body of work, summarised in his book *"The Social Causes of Depression in Women"* (1978) represents a challenge to the medical illness concept of depression. He showed that depression was a reaction to what was going on in the women's lives. Incidentally he also showed the high levels of stress, difficulty and hardship that characterised the lives of women living in London in the 1970s. His account is far more graphic than any psychiatric text in illustrating the level of suffering and disadvantage that is the background to psychiatric illness. There is a way in which clinical descriptions of psychiatric syndromes are just that - clinical. They separate out the life and experience of the person from their mental problem.

Studies of life events have been done in many countries, with many different psychiatric conditions. There is some evidence that different kinds of events lead to different kinds of symptoms. Losses and events with long term negative implications tend to produce depression: events leading to uncertainty and threat tend to cause anxiety and sudden occurrences that are upsetting and disturbing may cause psychosis.

The idea of 'cause' is complicated. Do the events cause the psychosis, or just precipitate it? This is a deep question that is often asked. If the person has had repeated episodes of psychosis then the importance of one event may be limited, but what if it is a first episode? There might be reason to think that someone was vulnerable all along. If one believes in the illness model then the assumption is that there was vulnerability from birth. So far, in the absence of any biological marker, there is no way of proving this in any individual case. Events certainly cannot explain all episodes of mental illness, and they may play a lesser part in those who have had recurrent episodes.

Brown went on from looking at factors that produce depression, to factors that lead to recovery. (Brown G 1988) The ideas were developed from in-depth studies of hundreds of women in London, over many years. They were able to work prospectively, interviewing women with long standing depression, identifying their problems, and then going back after they had recovered to see what had changed. This avoided the bias that creeps in when people are asked about their past. They describe two types of positive events. "Difficulty-reduction" involves one of the main causes of a person's depression being removed or neutralised. "Fresh-start events" involve a situation where there is reason to hope for better things. Such events may themselves involve considerable stress and threat, yet also "a sense of hope inherent in the situation, that life has taken some new turning, or that there is a chance to restore something lost." Examples of fresh-starts quoted by Brown are taking a new job, having a new confidant, having a new lover and returning to live with the family after being widowed.

One of the features of life events is their unpredictability. They tend to occur at a certain rate, but they are not the outcome of medical intervention. One of the strange features of life in an institution such as a hospital is that it cuts people off from real life. They are in the one place where they are removed from the unpredictable events of their life. It is a very "clinical" existence, where people do not transact business or form new relationships. The lack of events contributes to the restricted lives of those living there. This means that descriptions of how people got on over long periods in closed institutions, which used to be taken as illustrating the "natural history" of illness, are really describing people in one of the most unnatural places in the world. They are in a place where they are removed from many factors which could contribute to recovery.

4) Employment

Work is very important for maintaining morale and self-esteem. Being unemployed puts people more at risk of developing a mental health problem, and returning to work can play an important part in recovery. In the U.K. over 80% of those with serious mental health problems are unemployed. This is in marked contrast to the situation in poorer countries where being unemployed is less clear-cut. In a non-wage, subsistence economy people can return to whatever level of activity they are suited to. They do not face the hurdles of having to impress an employer, keeping regular hours or generally fitting in with a demanding role. When the WHO were carrying out a follow-up study of people suffering from schizophrenia in India it was found that the patients were often too busy working to keep appointments, men in the fields, and women with domestic work. This would not happen in the UK where unemployment is the norm, and until recently had been accepted as unavoidable. This was particularly the case at a time when unemployment was running at high levels in the U.K, but has persisted even though unemployment rates have fallen. There is now a renewed interest in helping people to get back to work. There are major obstacles however:

i) Financial disincentives.
   The benefit system makes it very difficult for people to re-enter work. In many cases they will be worse off than they were on benefit. This removes incentive, and one of the main purposes of returning to work.

ii) Low stress threshold
   Many who are recovering from mental health problems are very sensitive to stress, yet this is now a feature of nearly all jobs.

iii) Stigma

There have been a variety of schemes to help people get back to work. Industrial Therapy, which began in the 50s and 60s involved providing simple work as a way of getting back into normal routines. It was mainly aimed at people who had spent long periods in hospital. It was sheltered from normal economic forces and the workers were not paid a wage that they could live on. It was a positive innovation in its day and helped many people build up a life outside hospital. Now the idea of such separate and segregated arrangements is not widely accepted as a good idea. However it is worth remembering that employment at a humble and basic level played a decisive part in rehabilitating people who had suffered from long periods in hospital.

Supported employment schemes involve giving help to both worker and employer to get someone established back at work. The support may be for a limited period, or it may continue. Achieving open employment can have such far-reaching benefits that it justifies major investment in the process. However getting a job remains a major difficulty facing people trying to recover. Improved wages and working conditions have not made it easier for people to get back into work, because entry requirements have increased. It used to be suggested that people start with a job that is not too stressful and demanding. Now there are very few jobs of which this can be said.

The old idea of recovery is a barrier to employment as it tends to make people think that they should not consider work until they have "really" recovered. They end up on indefinite leave, waiting for this mythical state to arrive, all the time losing confidence and self-esteem. It is necessary to go back to work when one is not feeling 100%, and for this one needs active help from one's employer. This can sometimes be obtained, but is often not forthcoming. A culture of assisting people back to work is essential if the 80% not working is to be changed.

5) Shock

Joanne

Joanne was suffering from recurrent bouts of extreme agitation. She became convinced that she must kill herself, but when she attempted this she failed and ended up in hospital. She then had what she described as months of torment, being detained on a locked ward, and monitored night and day to make sure she could not harm herself again. She kept up her struggle against the system, in the end becoming careful to conceal her feelings from her captors. After careful planning she managed to throw herself out of a second storey window onto the concrete path below. Her injuries were surprisingly minor, but a fractured vertebra meant that she had to lie still for several weeks. I met her at that time and found her remarkably calm and happy. She said that when she woke up after her fall her life had changed. She could now describe the preceding months, as though talking about somebody else, someone she had been observing closely. She was now relieved of the distress that had so nearly killed her, and felt warm and loving towards the family who she had previously refused to see. I was in touch with her for several years, and there was no return of her agitation.

Such cases, and I have heard of many over the years, are tantalising. There is no shortage of theories that will be presented to explain the good outcome. However the theories were no help before the event, and are little use to all those who commit suicide without any dramatic recovery taking place. If recovery is so chancy and fickle how can anyone attain it?

One of the findings that Brown (1988) made about recovery from depression was that some of the "fresh-start" events were distinctly unpleasant. He described one woman who began to get better after a depression that had lasted for four years. She had had to have an emergency operation, after which the surgeon had said to her that she was "the luckiest girl in the world to be alive today". She said that had a great impact on her, and that from that point she had started being more positive. She felt more easy and stopped worrying. She started cutting down on her diazepam, took driving lessons and planned a holiday in Scotland. Brown speculates about such cases saying that "It seems therefore that it may at times be possible to get into the habit of depression, and some jolt is needed to give a more positive perspective on life, and a sense that one is needed as a person."

This kind of thinking has appealed to generations of preachers, teachers and therapists. They make a point of challenging, confronting, and pointing out shortcomings. There is a moral fervour that finds expression in shock tactics. There is a primitive moral stance that says in order to recover one must confess, admit one's weakness. This may be dressed up as a psychological approach, which focuses on the need to face up to things, to confront painful memories, and to talk about things you would prefer to keep to yourself. There is a hidden assumption here that psychiatric problems are due to a sort of moral weakness; a cowardice that prevents people facing up to things.

The deliberate use of shock to try to get people to recover is not recommended. One reason it fails is that the message can easily come over as critical; so that rather than give hope it does the opposite. In trying to shock someone out of their stuck condition there will always be a tendency to exaggerate, to impress. The subject will pick this up. It is received as a sort of bullying, and produces a negative response. The victim tends to become more entrenched.

A more sophisticated type of shock that is used by some therapists is the paradox. Here someone is given advice that is the opposite of what they might have expected. Instead of being urged yet again the control some compulsive behaviour they may be encouraged to do it even more than before. This is supposed to alter the forces that have been driving the behaviour, and make it easier for the person to take control.

Many interventions have unexpected consequences. I have often been told by people who have recovered that what changed things for them was not good treatment or advice but awful, bad treatment. Many have said that the experience of going into a psychiatric ward was so shocking that they determined to do everything in their power to leave and never return.

My conclusion is that people sometimes move on in their life following an unexpected shock, but that you should be wary of anyone who proposes this as a way to help someone. You should be wary of their motives as too often the shock option is just a way of dressing up irritation and frustration. It may be presented as a clever psychological intervention, but the recipient is likely to see it for what it is.

6) New interests

A number of people have reported the taking up of new interests as important to their recovery. Like the earlier items this may be something that come unexpectedly. One woman recovered from her long-standing depression when she had to look after her seriously ill son. He returned home and had to be nursed for months on end. Another woman was able to overcome years of depression and grief that followed the death of her husband when she had to start overseeing the family business.

These examples are both cases of demands being made on people, of being needed to fulfil a useful role. Neither was organised or planned as a route to recovery, but that is what they were.

7) Access to money and housing

The most obvious requirements for a secure existence can get forgotten in discussions of recovery. Absence of money and a place to live cause chronic stress and contribute to a tendency to have frequent relapses. In the past mental health workers were not good at helping people with these issues. Now money and accommodation can feature in anyone's care plan, and specialist help can be obtained. Debt counselling can make a great difference to people who otherwise face intractable problems. Far more can be achieved than a non-specialist might expect.

Accommodation options have been transformed in recent years, with many schemes to support people who prefer to live by themselves.

Positive conclusion

Many who have recovered stress that they had to take responsibility for their own recovery. For them, distancing themselves from the mental health services was an essential step. To allow oneself to be affected by natural change events is to take risks, and users of mental health services comment that professionals don't like risk. Yet, if one avoids all risk, life is likely to be dull and sterile.

Psychiatric intervention aims to preserve life, and where there is life there may be a change for the better. However what that change should be, and whether it is a risk worth taking, is entirely up to the individual.

Chapter 10
FALSE SOLUTIONS

Who is to say that a solution is false? This is a value judgment about what constitutes a good and worthwhile life. Some solutions, which may be criticised, may be all that was possible at the time. The options may become very limited to a person suffering from serious mental illness. To an outsider the choices made may seem perverse and misguided, but that generally reflects the outsider's inability to put them self in the place of the person concerned.

a) Suicide

Suicide appeals to many who suffer from mental illness. In periods of intense suffering it may be seen as a way out, a way to find peace. It may feature in psychotic thoughts that the person feels compelled to act upon. It may become quite suddenly a serious risk against which others have to protect the person. This is a common reason for someone to be detained in hospital under the Mental Health Act.

Many who are coming to terms with mental illness still think a lot about suicide. It is retained as an option, something that may be needed. Some describe suicide as something that gives them a sense of still having some control over their life. They hold onto the idea, and may even hold onto the means of committing suicide for the same reason. They remain ambivalent about it, not quite decided. If they wake up after a suicide attempt they may be pleased that they are now able to carry on. This living with suicide may explain the unexpected suicides that occur during recovery. The internal debate on the subject carries on, and may be swayed by a temporary setback. Suicide remains an option for people who are facing loss and disappointment.

During periods of acute mental turmoil thoughts of suicide are a sign of the need for urgent help. In our culture, the taboo on suicide means that it is rare for people to actively consider it unless they are experiencing acute mental distress. For this reason anyone who starts to express suicidal intentions is thought to warrant a psychiatric assessment. However for those living with, and coming to terms with mental illness, the taboo on suicide is lessened by long acquaintance.

My personal view goes along with current legislation. Anyone who has become mentally disturbed and is contemplating suicide is entitled to the best help that is available. It is a tragedy if people die in such circumstances. However there are people who face situations - such as loneliness, physical decline or loss of cherished hopes - which they are not prepared to endure. It is right that the offer of help is made to such people, and if necessary a period in hospital can be enforced. They may welcome help, which may restore their will to carry on. However suicide is not illegal, and if the best help available does not alter someone's outlook, then they should be able to decide their own fate. This is the law, yet it does not seem to be accepted. It is assumed that if anyone dies by suicide then someone is to blame.

During recovery, suicide is a real issue remaining close to the surface. People struggle with the problem on their own and may be relieved to have the chance to discuss it. There are always mixed feelings, and many will say that do not want to kill themselves, but they fear that they may. That opens the way to looking at measures that will help to keep the person safe. This involves simple matters like keeping in regular contact, anticipating periods of particular risk, and reducing access to anticipated methods. Just to have the conversation and make the plan is a signal that the situation is being taken seriously, and that one is committed to helping.

Loss of hope is a feature of most people who are depressed. They simply do not believe that things will ever improve. They may listen to you politely, but go away convinced that you were only humouring them. This grinding, complete and utter despair is often hidden behind a bland exterior, but is there if the right questions are asked. Communication needs to be very honest and open to avoid misunderstandings. Comments which may be intended to be light or humorous may be misunderstood by someone whose outlook is unrelievably bleak. It is worth making clear positive statements, and not leaving things unsaid. The fact that you can see a future for the person needs to be said, and expressed by involvement and commitment. If someone feels that they are of no value they can easily see what others do as confirming this. You have to be careful dealing with someone who is in such a sensitive state.

One unfortunate result of society's muddled thinking about suicide is that threatening suicide has become a common way of trying to influence people. It is a way in which people who feel themselves to be in a weak position can exert influence on people they see as being in a strong position. As is common in such scenarios the weak can then find it difficult to give up such a powerful bargaining counter. Some people who are recovering from mental illness can fall into this trap. It centres around power - the attempts of the weak to influence the strong. It is heightened by feelings of powerlessness and of a great power imbalance. It cannot be removed because such inequalities are a reality in the world. Awareness of what is happening and accepting that what people say is important will help. Without this awareness it is easy for such people to be seen as manipulative, and "having a personality disorder". Then negative readings of the situation can lead to further deterioration.

b) Alcohol and substance use and abuse

People recovering from mental health problems have the same tendency to rely on drugs and alcohol as the rest of the population. However they face a particularly challenging situation - so the risk is high.

Many who take cannabis claim that it helps them to relax. It is also said to help the uncomfortable side effects of antipsychotic medication. Most users are aware that it can lead to increased paranoia – but they accept this risk because of the perceived benefits. It is useful to consider that people taking such drugs are doing so for reasons – and not simply out of wilful self-indulgence. It may then be possible to work on an individualised programme to reduce the adverse effects of drug taking. Simply being critical of the practice and recommending programmes aimed at abstinence can be unhelpful.

There is evidence that cannabis can be a factor contributing to relapses in schizophrenia. In some individuals it may seriously undermine recovery plans. Here the raising of motivation and sharing of information are important. It is easy for a professional to adopt a lecturing or moralising tone, implying 'why do you have to be so stupid?' And 'why are you determined to make yourself ill?' Such sentiments are not usually said out loud, but come across quite clearly. Given the strength of medical opinion on these subjects these feelings are understandable, however I think they are entirely unhelpful and counterproductive.

c) Stuck in dependence on the Health Service

This has often been all that is available to people who have suffered from serious mental health problems, it has been the only plan on offer. With no work, and few social contacts, keeping in touch with the mental health service has been the only lifeline available. There has been a tendency to dismiss and sneer at such arrangements, and policy makers have been quick to close down old fashioned support services such as day hospitals, long before anything better was available. For those who have spent long periods in hospital, and have had their dependence actively encouraged, continuing support may be needed. However, there is a risk that people are offered an unnecessarily restricted existence – a sort of institutionalisation without the institution.

For the future it is hoped that services will be available to people when they need them, but that long term contact will be made in the wider community. A positive role of community workers would be to help people set up local activities. There is a shift towards a more limited role for the mental health services.

Chapter 11
TREATMENT, THERAPY AND RECOVERY

Treatment and therapy are the professional answers to what you need to help you to recover, but is this really true? Many people, myself included, make a living helping people recover, but which bits of what we do are really useful? If someone does well and gets better following treatment there can be an argument about whether it was the specific treatment that worked or the non-specific factors associated with treatment. Traditionally it is the specific treatments that get the credit. It is they that time, money and personnel are invested in. My contrary argument is that specific treatments may or may not make a contribution (they can also be frankly harmful), but it is the non-specific factors in treatment situations that have most potential to help people to recover.

Psychiatric treatments

The treatments favoured at any particular time will reflect current ideas about mental disorder, as well as the status and respect that are accorded to people with mental disorders. Those carrying out the treatments believe that what they are doing will aid recovery; a belief usually shared by those being treated.

Over the course of history just about anything that could be done by one person to another has been tried as a treatment for mental disorder. It is a sign of how difficult it is to tell whether a treatment is effective or not, that strange procedures which seem obviously unhelpful, have gone on being used for long periods in the past. Just because a treatment looks bizarre, cruel and harmful, does not mean it could not enjoy approval in a different age.

It is a continuous process - with the latest treatments coming to replace earlier ones. They have a more up to date rationale, are supported by recent studies; and have the backing of current leaders of opinion. So we are tempted to believe that now, at last, after all these generations, people have arrived at a clear "scientific" understanding of human nature. This leads to the illusion that the newest treatments are radically different from those available before. For example, earlier drug treatments are seen as ineffective, dangerous and likely to lead to addiction; whereas it is claimed that new treatments accurately correct the true underlying chemical disorder in the brain. Similarly, earlier forms of psychotherapy are seen as little better than dangerous hocus-pocus, leading patients to become stuck with their problems and dependent on their guru-like therapists; whereas cognitive-behaviour therapy which now leads the field, is seen as firmly based in the most up to date psychology.

Specific factors

In any treatment or therapy there are specific and non-specific factors. The claim made for a particular treatment is that it contains some specific ingredient which can produce change, and which is not present in other treatments. This specific factor is seen as having an effect on what is wrong with the person. It is linked to a theory of why the treatment should work. Outside psychiatry, for general medical conditions, treatment is directed to the cause of the illness. Doctors see making a diagnosis as the essential preliminary to treatment, because the diagnosis reveals what is causing the symptoms. Specific treatment can then eradicate or combat the pathological process; an infection can be treated, a cancer removed or a blocked artery cleared.

In psychiatry similar claims are made; that specific treatments can get to the causes of peoples trouble. For example, drug treatments are seen as altering levels of chemicals in the brain – those responsible for the mental disturbance; or different types of psychotherapy aim to uncover specific disturbances in how people think and how they relate to other people, seen as underlying their mental health problems. However the difference with psychiatry is that the "underlying causes" are theoretical, they can only be inferred from the presence of the symptoms.

Specific treatments are the kinds of interventions in which people put their faith. They often require special expertise and training for those who provide them. They feature strongly in books on psychiatry, and carry with them the authority of this specialist branch of medicine. There are cycles in which the popularity of different treatments rises and then falls. This is seen dramatically with drug treatment.

The image and public perception of a new drug is carefully managed by the company that produces it. It is presented as superior to the currently used drugs with impressive scientific papers and endorsements from leading professors. A lot of money is spent convincing the medical profession, even though at the time the drug is introduced there will be little hard evidence to go on, since not many patients will have been treated. The precise indications for the new drug will be a bit vague, but with good marketing it can enjoy a period of uncritical acceptance. Older drugs will be running into problems of side effects, or doubts about effectiveness – which make the new drug look attractive. Drugs can in this way come to occupy a leading position which they may hold for a number of years. However the cycle continues, and with longer use there are growing concerns about side-effects and effectiveness. The position of drugs earning large amounts of money is vigorously defended by experts and lawyers, contributing to the long time that it takes to get an objective view about how safe drugs really are. The same sort of legalistic practices used to defend any other commercial interest are employed by drug companies to defend the reputation of their product.

The cycle illustrates the fact that the popularity of prescription drugs depends on many factors other than scientific results. The marketing of drugs is sophisticated and costly, overshadowing the research costs. The consensus that develops among doctors about the usefulness of a drug is very carefully managed. So how can it be possible to form a genuinely balanced and informed opinion?

Similar cycles of fluctuating popularity can be seen with all specific treatments. In spite of this phenomenon, at any point in time, those working in the field tend to believe that the present treatments are effective. It causes embarrassment to raise the idea that maybe they are not. It causes cognitive dissonance to have a career in this field and not be convinced that the treatments being given are effective.

Null hypothesis

The null hypothesis, from which all discussions of effectiveness should start is that none of the treatments have specific actions. This would not mean that they are ineffective, but that on average, they are not better than placebos. In other words people improve but no more than they would if they had received a control treatment which would include the whole treatment package minus the specific active treatment. There are two difficulties in comparing a psychiatric treatment with a control:

1) It is difficult to devise control treatments in psychiatry because the subject can usually tell if they are not being given the active treatment. In drug trials subjects are given an inert substance instead of the drug, but they often realise this because of the lack of side-effects. If subjects realise that they are not having active treatment that will remove one of the powerful non-specific benefits that are present in normal treatment – namely the belief that you are being given something that will get you better. This could lead to a misleading result, with the active treatment doing better than the control, but not because it was a better treatment.

2) The normal treatment package, minus active ingredient, turns out to be remarkably effective. It contains a long list of non-specific factors and usually produces rates of improvement similar to active treatment.

If the null hypothesis were true, that would mean that the powerful forces that underlie placebo responding are enough to explain most or all treatment effects. A parallel idea is that the theories which back up the treatments are not true. What if our ideas about the working of the mind are no more "true" than those of Joseph Conolly 150 years ago? It will certainly look like that in another 150 years, probably sooner; unless one believes that recently developed theories of brain function are the last word on the subject. And Conolly didn't do so badly: he introduced humane guidelines which we are still not managing to put into practice.

If our specific treatments, on which people place so much faith, are not really effective; what then? Would that mean the end to hopes of helping people with mental illness? If I, as a psychiatrist, seriously put forward such an idea does it mean that I have given up completely – a burnt-out case? My thesis is quite the reverse. I believe that if we can distance ourselves for all the hype and exaggeration that surrounds particular theories and treatments, we would see more clearly how people recover and how they can be helped.

The Insulin Coma story

This is a well known story, from which I think there can be drawn an interesting conclusion. Insulin Coma was introduced as a psychiatric treatment by Sakel in 1933. (It is a feature of specific treatments that they usually have a name and a date attached to them. If the name is slightly exotic, so much the better.). It involved administering insulin, so that the level of blood sugar would fall and the person would go into a hypoglycaemic coma. The patient would then be revived by administering glucose. It was a difficult and risky business, requiring specially trained staff to carry it out. With some patients in mental hospitals it seemed to have good results, particularly those who were younger, with illnesses of recent onset. Some people, who had been withdrawn and apathetic, and were becoming stuck in hospital, improved so much that they were able to go home. The treatment enjoyed a brief period of being in fashion. New units were set up in many hospitals, with special teams of staff recruited. It seemed to be a valuable treatment in the attempts to move people on from long stay psychiatric wards.

There was a down side to the treatment. A number of people went into what were called "irreversible" comas. This meant that they did not come round from the coma when glucose was given, but remained unconscious for a long time – sometimes days or weeks. These individuals were likely later to be found to have suffered from brain damage during their coma.

In 1953, at the height of the enthusiasm for Insulin Coma, questions were raised about whether it was really effective. In 1957 a randomised controlled trial was carried out (one of the first ever), which showed that giving insulin to produce a coma was no more effective than a control treatment using a barbiturate drug to put people to sleep. After that the treatment gradually went out of fashion – partly because of the recent introduction of

116

chlorpromazine which was the first drug with antipsychotic effects.

This story is often presented as a triumph of scientific psychiatry over naïve optimism. It was one of the first demonstrations of the value of a controlled treatment trial. It showed that without science people will believe anything.

One cautionary conclusion is that during periods of therapeutic optimism doctors will overlook harmful effects of treatment – which if seen at any other time would cause immediate concern. My personal contact with insulin coma was second-hand, but none the less shocking:

Anna

Anna was well known to the hospital before I started working there. She had become a "revolving door" patient, who kept coming back, no matter what we did. She would become calm and settled in the hospital, and would then press to be allowed to leave. Then within weeks or months she would present again, usually in a severely deteriorated condition. She would be restless and agitated, unable to keep still or to express herself. She would be very irritable and often got drunk and injured in fights. She behaved so badly that as her repeated admissions continued, sympathy for her fell away. It came to be said that she was an alcoholic, or that she had a personality disorder, both conditions which at that time were not regarded as susceptible to hospital treatment. There came a point when people began to say that if that was how she was going to behave, she could not expect the services to bail her out every time that she got into trouble. This was an unfortunate development, common at that time, with the "untreatable" ending up as the "not deserving of treatment" As time went on the calm periods in hospital were less frequent and her distress greater. Then one day, shortly after yet another admission to the acute ward, she succeeded in hanging herself. I again had the job of writing a report for the coroner. To do this I sent to the archives for all her old notes. Then I learnt more about Anna than I had ever known during her lifetime.

She had had an unhappy childhood, from which she had escaped at the age of seventeen into a violent marriage. She then had a series of miscarriages before ending up being admitted to the psychiatric hospital in a regressed and dejected state. She was described as withdrawn and un-communicative by the ward staff. That may be why she was given insulin coma treatment. There were meticulous records of her treatment. Doses of insulin given, her response, including pulse, blood pressure and level of consciousness, and time to regaining consciousness were all recorded. The treatments had continued every day for many weeks. Then it appeared she had suffered from an irreversible coma. She had taken over twelve hours to regain consciousness, after which she was reported to be confused, disorientated and unable to stand. There was a brief note some time later from a physician who had examined her and found her to have weakness in one arm and leg which he thought was due to brain damage. There was no further note about her physical state until she was discharged from hospital many months later, at which time a brief note stated that she had had an abnormal reaction to insulin. What was clear to me was that her later life had been overshadowed by the brain damage that she had suffered.

The cautionary message from this story is obvious. Therapeutic enthusiasm can blind people to the harmful consequences of what they are doing. There is an excitement that can develop around a new treatment. Psychiatry is dangerously dependent on the claims made for today's treatments.

A more sober, but positive message from the insulin coma story is that people were being helped, they were moving on – but this had nothing to do with the strange new treatment. The improvements were the result of raising expectations, and encouraging staff to think that their patients could do better. The treatment units involved getting together teams of people, giving them a task and allowing them to devote extra attention to previously neglected patients. This is the neglected subtext every time dramatic claims are made about a therapeutic breakthrough. It shows that powerful forces can be directed towards helping people, but the nature of these is usually concealed behind some specific form of treatment, which gets the credit for benefits that occur. The real active ingredients are the interest, commitment and passion of those involved, and the new hope that they inspire. These are in addition to the placebo effects produced in the patients because of their belief that they will be helped.

Non-specific factors in recovery

Research in psychiatry is a constant struggle to distinguish genuine treatment effects from non-specific effects. Any claim that a treatment works has to prove that the observed benefits would not have occurred if an inert substance was used instead of the specific treatment being studied. The non-specific effects are the curse of the research industry. The most remarkable results are often greeted with scepticism, and exciting new treatments dismissed as "nothing more than placebos".

This background helps to explain why the medical profession is hostile and dismissive of placebos. The tendency of people to respond to seemingly inactive treatments can be seen as a regrettable human failing. However an alternative is to see it as central to an understanding of how people can recover. If placebo therapies miss out the ingredients that experts think are necessary, and placebo drugs lack any active chemicals at all, how can it be that they are so effective? In trials of all treatments the researchers are hard-pressed to show that their specific measures are any better than control treatments. Yet if the theories used to justify the specific treatments were true, then the control treatments would amount to nothing at all.

Non-specific factors include –

1) Positive expectations
Belief that treatment will work. Placebo responding is seen as dependent on this. Expectations can be enhanced and manipulated by a doctor, but also depend on past experience of similar treatment. Treatment and the role of the doctor in providing it may be part of the culture and traditions of society.

2) Contact with a support system
Being accepted as a sick person, and given special consideration such as time off work, sick pay and lightening of responsibilities. Being able to leave a stressful situation. Being supported in dealing with outside agencies. Being directed to sources of advice

3) Positive human values

Being dealt with by people who show human qualities such as altruism, optimism, hope, kindness, consideration, acceptance, toleration and patience.

These qualities are often in short supply in the situations in which people develop mental health problems. Families can be worn down by long periods of difficulty, and deteriorating relationships can lead to a vicious cycle of decline.

4) Individual support

As a crisis develops, lack of the most basic necessities can make any improvement impossible. Shelter, safety, food and clothing can all make a great difference. If their supply is in doubt, the whole future will look bleak.

5) Human contact

This involves someone having time and being available. It does not amount to therapy, but does require sensitivity, common sense and the ability to be a good listener. Many kinds of interaction may help, including:

Simply providing company, personal contact:

Being accepted as worthy of help

Being treated as interesting and likely to benefit

Being listened to

Being able to tell one's story

Being helped to gather one's thoughts

Working out an understanding of what is going on

Being treated with calmness, kindness and consideration

Ability to talk to others with similar experiences

6) Restoration of health

Deteriorating general health often undermines mental health.

Therefore steps to restore health are vital. These are not difficult or technical, but do need attention: the need for rest and sleep, healthy eating and drinking, and help with any difficulty that comes from cutting out drugs and alcohol. General health problems need attention as these may have been neglected, and may be a cause of psychological distress. Medication can help the person to calm down and sleep.

These factors are present to varying extents in many situations where people get help. They are the most powerful factors helping people to recover, yet they tend to be taken for granted – to such an extent that they pass unnoticed. If these matters are attended to they will make a big contribution to recovery, and if they are neglected recovery may not occur. The focus of attention of specific treatments may mean that the non-specific factors are neglected.

Evidence based medicine is a movement that aims to make sure that treatment is based on research findings wherever possible. It reinforces the idea that the priority in helping people is to get the right specific treatment. For any non-specific measures one might suggest, the answer is likely to be "there is no good evidence". Thus the importance of sleep, food, kindness, talking, and all sorts of common sense measures, is devalued. To be preoccupied with such things tends to be seen as a bit quaint and old-fashioned.

Drugs and talking treatments are the most important specific measures. They are the main focus of attempts to provide help, and this has the effect of diverting attention away from non-specific measures. Their benefits are difficult to assess because powerful pressure groups devote themselves to systematically exaggerating their value.

Chapter 12

DRUG TREATMENT IN PSYCHIATRY

Central role of drugs in psychiatry

Any review of the potential of psychiatry for aiding recovery needs to focus on drug treatment. Drugs can play a vital role in recovery, yet many of those who might benefit reject them as an option. The subject suffers from a legacy from generations of coercion, exaggeration and misinformation.

In the past, psychiatric patients had limited human rights. Treatments were prescribed, and patients were expected to take them. Drugs can still be administered by force, and various forms of coercion are common. In the past, being able to overcome people's reluctance to take medication, and persuade then to take it was seen as a valuable skill. This is now beginning to change, with vigorous efforts being made to protect people's rights to make their own decisions. However there is a well established culture of expecting people to take medication, which will take a long time to change. It is difficult for people working in psychiatry to allow their patients to make up their own minds about medication.

For every major disorder in the ICD – the International Classification of Diseases – there is a recommended medication. This means that medication is part of the recognised treatment, and someone who says that they do not want to take medication will be seen as uncooperative. What is more, a psychiatrist who does not prescribe medication may be seen as negligent. Agreeing to take what has been prescribed is called "compliance", and achieving compliance is an aim of treatment. "Compliance therapy" uses psychological techniques to counteract the individual's reluctance to comply. Being compliant was seen as a sign of "having insight", so that not wanting to have drug treatment was a sign that you were unwell. The word 'compliance' is a relic from an earlier age when being compliant was thought to be a good thing. Psychiatrists are now aware that this is no longer considered to be a good idea, and there is less talk of compliance, and more of 'concordance'. This is a less one sided relationship, but 'educating' patients about the benefits of drugs is still part of the process.

One consequence of the leading position given to drugs is that if drugs are not recommended for someone's treatment, then the conclusion that is drawn is that they must not really have any serious problem. It is difficult to make the case for offering intensive help from a psychiatric service if drugs are not included. If I, as a psychiatrist, am looking after a patient in hospital and I stop all their medication, serious questions will arise about why that person needs to be in hospital. This is confirmed by audits of people leaving psychiatric hospitals, which find that it is rare for a patient to be on no medication. This is in spite of the fact that many of those admitted have a history of dependence of drugs, or have tried to kill themselves with them.

It is against this background that conflicting ideas about medication should be considered. The medical case convinces most doctors that drugs are helpful for most patients. This leads to prescribing as a routine, which means that nearly all patients end up on drugs. This will include those who really don't like the idea of taking drugs, those who don't benefit, those who get serious side effects and those who do really well on them and have their lives transformed for the better. The antagonism that has been set up by the overuse of drugs turns many people against them and so effectively deprives them of the real benefits of medication. I think that it is necessary to become more aware of the risks and limitations of medication. This is not to say that nobody should take medication, but that the decision making process should be more careful, informed and shared. I remember that when I worked in a different field of medicine (rheumatology) patients would come to clinics with information that they had got from newspapers about new drugs. They were keen to try anything that would help them to get better. It was many years before I started to get similar requests in psychiatric clinics.

Example - Maintenance Treatment : the pros and cons

Maintenance treatment - the use of drugs to prevent future episodes of psychosis - is a good example of the difficulty in reconciling opposing views in this area.

The case for drug treatment – the pros and benefits

Following psychosis there is a high risk of relapse, especially for those whose lives remain difficult and stressful. Many studies have shown that remaining on antipsychotic medication, after the episode has passed, reduces the risk of relapse. This involves people who have got over their acute problems, people who appear well and back to normal.

Psychiatrists are very aware of the bad effect that a psychotic relapse can have on someone's life. They may lose their job, their relationships may break down and they may end up homeless and spending a long period in hospital. If things go badly a person may end up harming themselves or someone else. Psychiatrists have contact with people going through relapses every day of their working lives - so they are very aware of the risks. They may feel personally responsible if their patients relapse, and in the present adversarial climate they may be held responsible by some subsequent inquiry. They have the task of compelling people who have relapsed to come into hospital and accept treatment that they do not want. The wards in which they are responsible for people are often so bad that the psychiatrist may find it difficult to imagine what it would be like to be kept in such a place. The personal involvement of the psychiatrist in the process is reinforced by the fact that in all the legal procedures involving detained patients he is referred to as the RMO, the Responsible Medical Officer.

These considerations go some way to explaining why psychiatrists find it difficult to understand why someone would not accept treatment that was likely to prevent relapses. What is more this is treatment that is available, and deliverable. The research studies establishing the use of drugs in preventing relapses are among the core texts of modern psychiatry, produced by people who were leaders of British psychiatry. Psychiatrists are likely to feel that if anything is certain, in their difficult and contentious subject, it is the proven value of maintenance treatment to prevent relapses. All this makes the refusal to accept such treatment look wilfully perverse - or maybe the result of the self-same mental disorder that it is hoped to treat. As overt coercion is now unacceptable, compliance therapy, or "psycho-education" are seen as ways to overcome the irrational reluctance to take medication.

The case against drug treatment – the cons and costs

The antipsychotic drugs all have side-effects which can affect almost any aspect of a person's life. Each individual gets their own personal collection of side-effects, so that when they describe them to a doctor or nurse they are often met with scepticism and disbelief. The symptoms that people describe may be dismissed as not typical, or not known to be caused by that particular drug. However, longer acquaintance with this problem shows just how varied and wide-spread the harmful effects can be. They include:

a) Direct side-effects
Movement disorders which may be uncomfortable and disturbing, as well as giving the person an odd appearance. Such problems are very common.
Extreme restlessness, or akathisia, can be mistaken for a psychiatric disturbance requiring an increase in medication, which makes the problem worse. Tardive dyskinesia is particularly serious and disfiguring, and may become permanent.
Sexual dysfunction including impotence, problems with ejaculation, amenorrhoea and lactation.
Weight gain – almost universal, very difficult to do anything about.
Dysphoria - for many the worst effect. It can result in people not feeling normal while on the drugs. This effect tends to be played down in the literature, but it is not surprising since the prophylactic effect of the drug is meant to work by making people less responsive to things that go on around them.

b) Toxic effects
Some of the drugs produce potentially life-threatening effects in a percentage of those who take them. Lithium and clozapine are examples of this. To guard against this risk it is necessary to have regular health monitoring, including blood tests, as long as one is on the drug.

c) Stigma

Many are very aware of the stigma of being on long-term drugs. There is a common perception that it is a sign of weakness to have to continue to take medication. There are jokes about people needing medication, and "keep taking the tablets" is an insult. The result is that many feel that their self esteem suffers from having to stay on tablets, and that as long as they stay on them they will not be properly recovered. This leads many to stop medication, in unplanned ways, against advice, often with bad consequences.

d) Uncertainty of effectiveness remains

In spite of the strong medical consensus that prophylactic drugs are effective there are still opposing views. It turns out to be very difficult to devise any experimental study that will prove the case.

> i) There is a large placebo effect from being on a prophylactic drug. Such drug treatment is usually part of a package that includes regular meetings, monitoring of health – both mental and physical, and a certain measure of personal support. In the past most of the drugs used for relapse prevention were given by injection. This could lead to a particularly strong link being set up - which often continued for many years. I have found that it is almost impossible to get a service to provide an equivalent personalised long term support at home if having a drug administered is not part of the package. Such support may be offered, but it usually stops within weeks of the injections being discontinued.

> ii) If regular antipsychotic drugs are suddenly stopped, or in an experimental study switched to an inert substance, this tends to precipitate a psychotic episode. In other words, suddenly stopping the drug, which is intended to prevent relapses, can itself precipitate one. This has serious implications for the management of maintenance treatment. It means that stopping treatment is always going to raise the risk of relapse, so that if starting and stopping treatment is likely to occur, the treatment may do more harm than good.

iii) Maintenance treatment is said to reduce relapses, not abolish them.

iv) This treatment aims to make people less likely to react to stress by having a relapse into psychotic illness. It may make people more able to cope with stressful, adverse conditions. Many fear that such treatment puts too much emphasis on modifying the individual, and not enough on improving their lives.

v) Objective study of the effectiveness of maintenance treatment is difficult because this treatment is now so much part of standard practice that a trial without medication might well be considered unethical.

vi) Medical opinion is not unanimous. There is a view that taking antipsychotic drugs could make people supersensitive to dopamine, and so more prone to relapse. It has even been suggested that this may be part of the explanation for the lower relapse rates that have been found in poorer countries. These ideas are not widely accepted by psychiatrists, but they show that the subject is not as clear cut as it is presented.

How can decisions be made? Cost/ benefit analysis

With such opposing views, how can decisions about treatment be made? Cost/ benefit analysis involves weighing up costs against benefits, and deciding whether the treatment is worthwhile.

Costs –   risks to health
             unpleasant side effects
             inconvenience and financial cost
             dislike of taking medication, stigma

Benefits –   health gain
             improved social functioning

improved subjective experience

relapse prevention

In the past doctors were trained and expected to make such decisions. This was true throughout medicine, but especially so in psychiatry. Part of the craft that doctors learnt was the ability to do these calculations in their heads, and then prescribe what they considered to be the correct treatment. It is now accepted that those who are being treated should be helped to make their own decisions; but is this realistic?

The new term is "concordance", which means shared decision making, and arriving at an agreement which respects the wishes and beliefs of the patient. For this process to take place the person needs accurate and relevant information. They need good evidence about the costs and benefits of any proposed treatment. But how are they to get through the mass of information that is available? They can use the internet, drug information from manufacturers, information from self help groups, news letters from pressure groups and statements from government bodies such as NICE. How can anyone find their way through all this?

Psychiatrists have always seen providing information as part of their role, but in the past "patient education" was seen as a way of increasing compliance, rather than encouraging choice. Talk of education tends to assume that the educator knows the answers.

Evidence Based Medicine

Evidence Based Medicine (EBM) is " *The conscientious, explicit and judicious use of current best evidence in making decisions about the care of individual patients.*" (Sackett et al 1996). The volume of medical research is now so great that systematic ways are needed to find relevant information. The Cochrane Collaboration was set up to provide a database of the best available scientific results. The big claim that is made for EBM is that it is scientific, and can provide the information needed if informed treatment decisions are to be made.

EBM, which seems such a good idea, turns out to have limitations when you try to apply the results to help individual patients.

1) The first problem is that EBM is highly selective about what counts as good evidence. Randomised Controlled Trials (RCTs) are the main sources of information. These trials require groups of patients with defined, uncomplicated conditions, who are receiving standardised treatments. The trials exclude patients with complications such as substance use, forensic history or suicidal tendencies. This is an immediate problem since most patients treated by mental health services have complex problems. Trials therefore give limited information about the treatment of people with the types of complex problem commonly seen in NHS practice.

2) There is the problem of comparing what may be available locally with an ideal service that has been set up specifically to carry out a ground-breaking piece of research. The training of workers and their case-loads will be different. It must raise questions about the value of adding together large numbers of studies when one learns that 80% of the studies reviewed in EBM are carried out in the USA where the health care system and social structure are very different from those in the UK..

3) RCTs focus on certain types of specific intervention – the sorts of things favoured by academic departments and drug companies. Up to 2002, out of 96 reviews on mental health topics summarised, 88 dealt with specific drug treatments or therapies. This means that for all other aspects of care, not suitable for study by RCT, the conclusion from looking at the data base will be that "there is no reliable evidence". That has become the most damning phrase in psychiatry. It can cut the ground from under any number of bold and positive initiatives, and make them look much less well established than any sort of drug treatment. On drugs there is a vast amount of evidence – because there is a large industry producing it. On treating people with respect and kindness, there is nothing.

4) When large numbers of trials are added together the conclusion

that is reached is that drug treatment is undoubtedly effective. However, this argument is flawed because it is never known how many trials producing negative results fail to see the light of day. It is only those that get published that are counted. There is a strong financial incentive for drug companies not to publish negative results. For this reason there are now moves to make it compulsory for all trial results to be published. This would be a step towards reducing "publication bias".

5) The large number of drug trials produce surprisingly modest results. Most drugs turn out to be slightly better than placebos but probably no better than rival drugs. The differences between drugs that come out of EBM studies are of little help in deciding which drug will help a particular person. Of more interest to the patient is what side effects they will experience, or whether their combination of symptoms will be helped. He or she might also like to hear accounts of people who have taken the drug.

6) EBM studies claim to be objective and dispassionate. However it is naïve not to consider the likelihood of bias. The industry that provides the evidence makes billions of pounds from the drugs. A single bad report can ruin a drug, and the careers of those involved. In addition to unconscious bias, there is evidence that fraud is not uncommon.

7) Therapy trials are inevitably run by enthusiasts. They devote their lives to particular styles of treatment, and it is they who evaluate them. Studies will include "control" treatments, which lack the vital ingredient of their energy and commitment. How can someone delivering a control treatment possibly have the same enthusiasm as the person delivering the real thing?

Most of the EBM studies in mental health that do not involve drug treatments, are on the subject of ACT – Assertive Community Treatment. The positive results of these trials are regarded as a triumph of science. However here there is a major problem of what should count as a control. The usual answer is to compare ACT with 'standard care'. There is particularly likely to be a difference in enthusiasm and vigour between an exciting new team and an old one that has been left out of the modernising of services.

Another case where controls are difficult is CBT – Cognitive Behaviour Therapy, which has achieved a dominating position in the UK. A particular approach sometimes comes to occupy this position, and it makes people ask whether further trials are really needed, or whether it is ethical to put someone in a trial which might result in them not receiving CBT. There are plenty of trials showing how effective CBT is; but what do they use as a control? It is often either 'supportive therapy' or befriending; however these are usually carried out by cognitive therapists. There is a problem with what is called 'investigator allegiance'. If each study is open to this kind of criticism, the problem is not reduced by lumping together a whole series to produce an average result.

EBM sounds wonderful in theory, but in psychiatry its scope for helping in the individual decision is limited. It runs the risk of being a Trojan Horse, allowing medical paternalism back into the process. EBM is so complicated that only a trained person can understand what is said. How is a lay person to decipher the statistical jargon with which EBM is surrounded? Those who support EBM see it as a way of cleansing medicine from messy subjectivism. Its advocates use the results to produce protocols for treatment – so that decisions made will conform to "best practice". This however is only a short distance away from the old ideas of compliance – except now not only should the patient comply, but also the doctor.

Drug trials show only small differences in effectiveness between different drugs, which limits their usefulness in individual decision making. However where EBM could play a vital role is in picking up evidence that drugs are dangerous. In this it has not done well. A recent decision that the antidepressant Paroxetine should not be prescribed to people under the age of 18 was not a triumph for EBM but the outcome of a prolonged campaign by patients and families. This is one of the most widely prescribed psychiatric drugs, in use for over ten years. Rumours and reports circulated for years, but were always dismissed by experts from the industry. It was investigative reporters, television film makers and aggrieved families who finally persuaded the regulatory authorities to alter the official guidance to doctors. The same process has resulted in the belated advice that antidepressants are not recommended for mild to moderate depression. This sort of story does not increase confidence in EBM. There is a suspicion that all the science associated with drugs is directed primarily to commercial ends. It is a great and impressive edifice, but the driving force behind it is not a desire to help people.

EBM is about getting the best available information into the decision making process. However information is only part of the equation. The goal of concordance is that decisions should respect the beliefs and wishes of patients. This means that individual likes and preferences, beliefs and prejudices, are vital to the process. This goes against the spirit of how EBM is now being pushed in academic and government circles. There it is seen as the triumph of science over the individual's likes and dislikes. However, 'messy subjectivism' may be one of the things that human beings are stuck with.

The alternative to EBM – clinical judgment

The strongest argument in favour of EBM is that the alternative is even worse. The alternative is that decisions about treatment are based on something called "clinical judgment". This has always been the cornerstone of medical practice. Doctors gain experience through treating patients. They learn what works and what does not, based on:

What they remember of people they have treated.

How people have responded to treatment

Their training - which may be many years ago

Effects of influential people e.g. professors, drug reps

A lifetime of experience (and prejudice)

Personal and family experience

These sources of learning lead to the development of clinical judgment. Individual doctors may have particularly good judgment, and be good at advising patients. However clinical judgment can also be used to justify any narrow, limited or plain wrong approach that a doctor wishes to follow. As an approach to making decisions using large amounts of information, it is hard to defend. It may have worked in the past, but the sheer amount of information now available makes it unreliable.

The chloramphenicol story illustrates the risk of relying on clinical judgment. Chloramphenicol is an antibiotic which was very good at treating a variety of infections that were commonly met in general practice. Its use came to an abrupt end when it had to be withdrawn after it was found to cause a fatal blood disorder in about one out of every 2000 people who took it. You could have been a General Practitioner using it as your favoured treatment for common infections throughout your entire career and you might have retired without coming across any problems with it. That is how clinical judgment worked in the past. Doctors became familiar with certain treatments, they would swear by them, and go on using them – often until stopped from doing so. The Insulin Coma story did not come to an end in 1957 when the RCT was published. Enthusiasts went on using the treatment for years. They had faith, and personal investment, in it. If you are a doctor on your own, treating the patients who come to see you, you are at great risk of being strongly affected by one or two cases. If you give a drug to someone and they make a dramatic recovery and are very grateful, there is a danger that you will go on giving that drug to people for years – in the hope of achieving the same result; there will always be the nagging doubt that maybe the drug had nothing to do with what happened anyway.

So the problem remains – how can a decision be made about what treatment is right for an individual. EBM may give broad answers about treatments which may be effective. It would be helpful if it gave more definite help in uncovering treatments that are dangerous. However, when it comes down to making the decision about treatment for one particular individual, a cost – benefit analysis has to be carried out. This involves a careful weighing up of pros and cons. This may look like a scientific matter, but it is not. It depends on value judgements. It is a question of what a person wants, what risks they want to take, what discomfort they are prepared to tolerate, and what their priorities are. It also needs to reflect their cultural and ethical values. In the past it was customary to say that treatment decisions were too technical for a lay person to understand. This overlooked the fact that beyond the technical questions there are always value judgements. And now it is clear that the lay public is quite capable of understanding the science involved – provided it is explained.

The debate about maintenance drug treatment to prevent relapses of psychotic illness illustrates some of the conflicts. Psychiatrists are often appalled at the idea that people risk having a psychotic episode rather than take regular medication. They may attribute such views to mental illness and can seek legal ways to override them. Yet it is still a value judgment, all about what is important to the person, and what it is like to be a person taking regular medication.

The problem with "concordance" and shared decision making is that sharing will often be a fraud. EBM strengthens psychiatrists in the belief that they know what is right for people. Even if they are very liberal-minded, and inclined to go along with what people want, they will fall foul of protocols and government directives. If the psychiatrist thinks he knows what the right treatment is, how can he be involved in setting up the wrong treatment? The problem here is the idea that psychiatry has reached a point where there is a scientifically correct answer to every individual person's problems. This goes to the heart of the matter. There is no right official route to recovery. Each individual's problems can be tackled in several different ways, it is just arrogance to say that the professional's answer is the only correct one.

User directed drug treatment

One solution to the problem is that decisions about treatment should be made by those being treated, unless there is some good reason why they should not. This may seem, on the face of it to be a very bad idea. Surely doctors are paid to make decisions about treatment. How can people possibly know what is the right treatment? To many people it will be seen as a total abdication of responsibility for doctors to ask patients what treatment they want. However, individual likes and preferences play an important part in most treatment decisions; they can not be decided by objective criteria alone. If the person does not direct their treatment, then it will be directed by a doctor who will have to make assumptions about the person's interests and attitudes.

In some circumstances it may seem that there is little room for debate. "Rapid Tranquillisation"(RT) is an example of this. It is an emergency procedure used to calm the behaviour of someone who is dangerously agitated and out of control. It is often carried out on people who have been detained in hospital under the Mental Health Act, and it may be carried out in spite of their not consenting to it. It might seem that there is little scope here for User Directed Drug Treatment. However those who have been on the receiving end of RT usually develop strong feelings and opinions about it. There are always a number of different procedures that can be followed – different drugs, different doses, different routes of administration, and different nursing procedures for the administration of the medication. In the past all these treatment decisions were jealously guarded as areas for professional judgement. However there is very little justification for this, and allowing the person to make decisions about their treatment is vital if they are going to regain control of the situation. It is precisely in situations like this, where people are at their most vulnerable, that they may develop negative reactions to being given medication.

At times of crisis it may be very difficult for a person to get their views across. Various ways have been developed to get round this. One way is for their care plan to include their preferred options, should urgent treatment be required. This can also be put on a Crisis Card that the person carries, or more formally they may write an Advance Directive. These can exert an influence over treatment, even if they are not legally binding. It is important to acknowledge the limitations of advance directives so that people are not disappointed. It is not possible to specify treatment which would be unethical or practically impossible. It would be reasonable for someone to say that they would prefer to be treated at home, but not that they must never again be detained under the Mental Health Act.

Information and evidence are necessary if people are to make decisions about their treatment. There is not usually any shortage of information, the difficulty is weighing it up. A particular problem arises with drugs and their possible side effects. Doctors are supposed to warn patients about side effects before they prescribe medication – but how much should they say? The drug information leaflets provided by the manufacturer list many serious and frightening side effects for every drug. The effect of this is to make the information unintelligible. If a doctor is recommending a drug which is said to cause total hair loss, skin disease, epileptic fits and sudden death what is the patient to think? If the doctor mentions side effects they are usually part of a discussion which ends with the doctor recommending that the person takes the drug. The implication must be that the side effects are not too bad.

One interesting development is that sometimes the Committee on the Safety of Medicines (CSM) becomes concerned about a side effect and instructs doctors to carry out special monitoring of patients who take the drug. For example, this happened with the antipsychotic Pimozide, and people who are taking it must now have ECG monitoring. This makes it obvious that a serious level of concern has developed about the drug and it has the effect of putting doctors off prescribing that drug. At present there is much concern that the antipsychotic drug Olanzapine causes raised blood sugar levels, which can lead to diabetes. It is still possible to prescribe that drug, mentioning the risk but saying that on balance it is still recommended. If the CSM made a rule that people put on Olanzapine have to have their blood sugar monitored, that is likely to put people off taking (and prescribing) it. How can anyone be happy with a drug which may give them diabetes? The answer is that they may not be happy but it may be a choice that someone is able to make. It is certainly not a choice that someone else can make for you.

Pharmacists can play an important role in providing people with information about drugs. There are pharmacists who work in the mental health field who are experts in the drugs used in psychiatry. They are not involved in prescribing decisions and so have a more objective position. This makes them able to advise both doctor and patient about options for treatment.

Non-specific effects of drugs

Drugs have been used for thousands of years to calm people and to relieve mental distress. There are a number of beneficial effects of drugs which do not rely on any particular theory about mental illness. Many of those who seek help have symptoms which can be helped in this way. These symptoms include agitation, difficulty sleeping, restlessness, over-arousal, and preoccupation with distressing thoughts. They can easily lead to a vicious cycle in which increasing symptoms lead to progressively more disturbed and dangerous behaviour.

Drug intervention can be aimed at improving sleep, reducing arousal, calming, reducing the impact of disturbing thoughts, and allowing rest and relaxation. A wide range of drugs can achieve these aims. This will include tranquillisers, antidepressants, antipsychotics, anticonvulsants, hypnotics, opiates, alcohol, and many other groups. All have things in their favour, and things against. The point is that drugs can be very useful at a purely symptomatic level, without any reference to complicated theories about disturbances in brain chemicals causing mental illness.

In practice doctors are often inhibited from giving helpful, non-specific, drug treatment by their attachment to particular theories. For example many people present in a distressed state, feeling hopeless and unable to carry on. They are often agitated and desperate from lack of sleep. They ask directly for something to help them rest and sleep. However what they are often given is a drug that is intended to treat their depressive illness, such as fluoxetine (Prozac) or paroxetine (Seroxat). These drugs may in fact make insomnia and agitation worse. The medical idea is always that you shouldn't be treating symptoms, but rather the "underlying illness". This is what I am questioning. Helping people should begin with listening to what they are actually complaining about.

Specific effects of drugs

Drugs can play an important role in combating symptoms and alleviating distress. They can therefore be important in the achievement of recovery. There are particular types of symptoms which are helped by particular drugs. Any recommendations have to be very general because individual response is so unpredictable. It also has to be remembered with any particular drug given to any individual that there may be a less than 50% chance that it will be helpful. This means that it is essential to monitor response from the start. Too often people are left on drugs that are not helping, or even have the doses increased. If a drug is not doing someone any good it is quite likely to be doing them harm.

Antipsychotics

These can produce remarkable improvements for people suffering from symptoms such as hallucinations, delusions and paranoia. They may take several weeks to have their effect, and the reduction in symptoms may be gradual. This time delay can be difficult as everyone may become convinced that the drug is not working. The delay can lead to pressure to increase the dose, which can make side-effects much more of a problem.

The antipsychotic drugs remain the most important and clear-cut of all the drug treatments, they can literally transform lives. However they do not work for everyone, and many who could benefit do not take them.

Different drugs in the group have different side effects, and all can be serious. These are very important because if someone suffers from bad side effects they may be put off taking medication for ever. For this reason they should never be played down. I have often seen people being reassured that some problem that has developed is not a side effect - simply because it is not one of the most typical and well-known ones. In fact side effects are very varied, and often unexpected and odd.

Newer "atypical" antipsychotics have been strongly marketed on the basis that they have fewer side effects than the older drugs. This is true and they are now regarded as the first line in treatment, especially for someone having treatment for the first time. Low dose regimes can help to get treatment started without producing unacceptable side-effects. As time goes on there is growing awareness of unwanted effects from newer antipsychotics - which reinforces the need for continued vigilance. The atypical antipsychotics are expensive drugs, and a lot has been spent on marketing them. Older antipsychotic drugs are still available, but there is little interest now in research into low-dose strategies using old drugs. This is unfortunate, because when they went out of favour they were being used in high doses, with high levels of side effects.

The doctor and patient have to work hard to establish a drug regime that suits the individual. There is little science to help with this, little to say what will help any particular individual. Psychiatrists have traditionally liked to select the drug that they thought most suitable for each individual. While they can recommend a drug this is not based on sound evidence. There is no reason why the patient should not be provided with the necessary information to make a decision, if he or she wishes.

In the case of Kate (Ch 1), I described how I treated her for several weeks, against her wishes, before she lost her symptoms. The treatment worked, but I later discovered that she had been left angry and unhappy about the whole process. I used this to make the point that symptomatic drug treatment is not the same as recovery. I still think I was right to treat Kate as I did. If I had not done so it is likely that her child would have been taken into care, and she would have placed herself at great risk. I was providing emergency treatment, not getting her to recover.

It is a big problem that those with serious and acute problems are often against the idea of taking any medication. This may be because they do not think that they have any kind of problem. So, what can be done?

1) Give it time. Talk it over several times, explain the rationale, answer questions, review past drug treatments; arrange to meet again.

2) Make clear that the drug is only one idea, and help will continue even if the offer is refused. If one drug does not have a good effect then another can be tried.

3) Think laterally, make sure there is more than one option on offer, consider low dose options.

4) It can help if the person talks to someone who is on the drug and has found it helpful.

5) Give it more time and explain what has led you to make the suggestion. Like other aspects of anyone's programme, medication should be a subject for ongoing dialogue.

6) Explain the Mental Health Act and how this may be used (since all who have serious mental illness may be affected by it, see Ch. 15). This is a difficult area and it is easy for people to feel that they are being bullied into taking medication. It is important to give straight information so the patient knows what their legal position is.

Some families, and others wanting to help someone become desperate about this subject. I have known families concealing drugs in a person's food out of desperation. This is not only unethical and probably illegal but likely to be counterproductive. In most people there is an internal debate that goes on, and too much pressure from outside is can push the argument the wrong way.

People who have been admitted to hospital under the Mental Health Act can be compelled to take medication. As a last resort they can be given injections against their will. Nobody likes this, but it not an uncommon practice. The circumstances in which this can be done are strictly controlled by the Mental Health Act. Compulsory treatment can lead to significant change within a few weeks, this may be enough to make it possible for the person to leave hospital. If medication has been helpful, and it is important to continue it, this will only happen if the person agrees to it. This means that the imposing of treatment has to be handled very sensitively, with the same discussion and information giving that would occur if the treatment was voluntary. If the person is turned against medication by their experiences, then they have been done a disservice, and the whole exercise may be counter-productive. If the law is changed to allow continued compulsory treatment, even after patients have left hospital, there is a danger that the imperative on teams to explain and justify their drug treatment may be reduced.

Home treatment is an alternative to admission for many people. It does require some measure of willingness to participate, but most people prefer it to admission. It can be a way to avoid a compulsory admission. Medication is a key part of the home treatment of acute episodes. It is possible for members of the team to visit several time each day to administer tablets. This can be very supportive, and allow the family not to be involved in this difficult task.

I have stressed the problems associated with drug treatment because

I think that glossing over these has done a disservice to those who could benefit. Treating psychotic symptoms with drugs will always be difficult, and will require a lot of attention to detail. Some people who have such symptoms may recover without the help of drugs. These will be those in the best outcome group, typically those with recent onset, acute symptoms and no major problems before the onset of symptoms. This is unfortunately a fairly small group. For most others, at some stage drug treatment is likely to be needed. Warner (2004) has done more than anyone to urge caution in the use of antipsychotic drugs, yet his conclusion is, "In practice, for most patients drug free treatment is not feasible." This is the situation in the UK. The evidence that drug free treatment is often successful in non-western countries does not seem to be relevant here.

Antidepressants

The case for antidepressants is less clear-cut. People with mild or recent depression are advised to wait and try some form of counselling or cognitive behaviour therapy (CBT) as a first step. If the depression persists, is severe or has psychotic features then drugs are recommended. There is a lot of evidence that many people who suffer from depression benefit from antidepressants, maybe 50-75% of those treated.

Many studies have shown that cognitive therapy is at least as effective as drugs for treating depression, and it has the advantages of reducing the relapse rate. Some studies show that there are advantages in people having both treatments together - therapy and tablets. The difficulty in evaluating cognitive therapy is that it meets many non-specific needs, so it is difficult to be sure that it is the therapy that is so effective. It gives people a lot of time with a therapist, it gets them to review their life and it gives a meaningful explanation to what has happened to them. Antidepressants are often all that is offered by general practitioners, because they do not have access to other treatments. The recommendation that talking treatments should be the first approach will often fail because they are not available.

In NHS psychiatry, where people tend to have complicated problems with difficulties in several areas of life at once, the benefits of antidepressants are less clear. This is especially the case for those depressed people who end up being admitted to hospital. Their complex problems will need to be addressed by a comprehensive care plan, and putting too much faith in an antidepressant may not be helpful. A further complication in hospital psychiatry is that most people who are referred with any kind of mood upset are already taking antidepressants. In fact they may well have been on a succession of antidepressants for several years. Then the question is, should the drug be changed – to maybe to a "newer" one? The chance of this being a decisive intervention are low, and it is best if people do not put all their faith in the drug making them better. There are many other measures that may be more important.

Some people react badly to antidepressants. Some of the SSRI drugs seem to stimulate, causing an increase in brain activity. For some this may be just what they want. However, for many who are full of angry, bitter, destructive thoughts, those thoughts may increase in intensity. This can result in a sudden worsening of the patients condition with the emergence of apparently new symptoms, in particular suicidal and homicidal thoughts. People should be aware of this and not persevere with the drug if they are getting worse. In hospital practice I have often seen people who have been referred because their condition has suddenly deteriorated, and careful history taking shows that the change followed starting a new drug. The connection between the new drug and the worsening symptoms is often not noticed, and the dose of the drug may actually have been increased.

Older antidepressants such as the tricyclics do not cause this problem, but they have their own severe drawbacks - including dangerous toxicity if taken as an overdose. Since many consult precisely because they are becoming suicidal this is a major problem.

My conclusion is that antidepressants work best for those with less complicated problems – rather as Sargant said in 1966! There are no strong guidelines to say which depressed people will respond and which will not, and no sound basis to prefer one drug to another for a particular person. This view is heresy to many psychiatrists who pride themselves on being able to say whether or not drugs will help, and which is the right drug. However I don't think there is any sound science behind it. The question is whether someone wants to try an antidepressant, and then deciding on one on the basis of what is known.

As with antipsychotics, there is an awful lot of science, but it is still up to the doctor and patient to work out what is suitable for the individual. The official story is that antidepressants are for defined courses of treatment, after which they should be stopped. The advice is that the drugs should continue for 3-6 months after the symptoms have improved. That makes for a very long time on the drugs. Then there are withdrawal effects experienced by many on stopping – odd unexpected symptoms including dizziness, nausea and shocks in the body. The withdrawal effects stop after a week or two, but make it difficult for some to stop the drugs. The withdrawal syndrome has now appeared in patient information leaflets, about ten years after people started experiencing it, and being told they were imagining things.

It is not surprising that stopping and starting drug treatment is difficult, especially if one believes the claims made for the drugs. They are said to correct certain chemical imbalances in the brain, which are themselves the cause of the symptoms. Taking the drug restores the brain chemistry, so that the symptoms go. With the brain now functioning with the benefit of the drug, it is difficult to see how it is supposed to manage when the drug is stopped. Suddenly stopping the drug is likely to cause a very severe upset – and it is now acknowledged that this is true. The answer is that drugs need to be reduced very slowly, over months rather then weeks. There are still risks that there will be a return of depression after the drug is stopped. This may lead to restarting the drug and then the person being understandably reluctant to stop. The reality is that a lot of people end up taking the drugs for long indefinite periods. This is now sanctioned by drug experts who say that long term treatment is justified for recurrent depression. An alternative view is that being unable to come off the drugs is a further problem that can follow taking them, and this should be considered before starting.

Mood stabilising drugs

These drugs are used for people with recurrent mood disorders. Their use is complicated and starting one of the drugs is a major undertaking. It will involve long term contact with a clinic, regular appointments, and taking a drug every day, even though the person is entirely well. For lithium there is the need for regular blood tests because of the risk of toxic effects if the blood level is too high. Many people take these drugs and are convinced that they keep them well. Many others start them, forget to take them, and stop them, and for them the drugs may do more harm than good.

To get on well with these drugs it is necessary to be regular, reliable and fully committed to the programme. The clinic visits may be supportive, and the whole package appreciated as an insurance against relapse. It can be argued that it is the non-specific elements in the package which make the difference. Going onto the drug and signing up for the clinic is a very positive step to bring one's life under control. Scientists continue to debate how much the actual drugs contribute, but I am sure the package as a whole is helpful for many. Unfortunately it is not helpful for those whose lives are too chaotic to take the drugs regularly, have the blood tests and attend the clinic. Since starting and then stopping the drugs increases the risk of relapse, such people should be steered away from these drugs.

These drugs are also used for the acute treatment of manic episodes. This is helpful in reducing the need for heavy use of antipsychotic drugs. However if the person is not committed to staying on the drugs long term, stopping them at the end of treatment may cause problems. As with antipsychotics, going on these drugs has to be approached carefully. Too often people end up on them in hospital, without preparation.

Tranquillisers

The benzodiazepine drugs are widely used for treating anxiety, and they are also used in hospital for treating psychotic episodes. However they have had such a chequered history that doctors find it difficult to prescribe them rationally. During the 1970's and 80's they were over-prescribed so that many people developed chemical dependence on them. For those people getting off the drugs was a long and painful process, not helped by the fact that for a long time the medical profession denied that there was any problem. The drugs reduce the sensations of panic and anxiety. Where these symptoms are severe and incapacitating the drugs can be very effective – in a proportion of people. However people quickly get used to the drugs and become dependent on them. For this reason they are not recommended for more than short term use. Within these limits the drugs are effective, but the bad history means that doctors often avoid them, and offer less suitable drugs for acute anxiety.

There are still people who have been taking benzodiazepines for years on end. There are ways of helping them to come off the drugs, but these are all slow, time-consuming and painful. That explains why some are not keen to stop. If people are suddenly taken off the drugs, which sometimes happens from the misguided actions of doctors, they can become acutely disturbed.

Stopping drug treatment

This is a difficult and contentious subject. The official version of what happens is out of step with reality. The illness-treatment-recovery model, leads to the idea that drugs treat episodes of illness, after which they should be stopped. In fact, once established on medication, stopping is never easy. People become accustomed to taking drugs, and understandably nervous about stopping. They then may react badly if they experience an increase in symptoms around the time they stop the drug. They may well think that they are suffering from a relapse – and so feel that they should go back on the drug. Most drugs have a "discontinuation syndrome"; a group of symptoms which occur when the drug is stopped. These occur in a person who is already anxious.

Theories that back up drug treatment are moving towards the need for long term, i.e. indefinite treatment. It is argued that depression, like schizophrenia, is a recurrent condition and long term drug treatment is needed. This seems to be recognition of the fact that many who respond to antidepressants will relapse when they are stopped, so that there are now many people on the drugs on a long term basis. One response to this problem is to make sure the issue of how long the drug will be taken is reviewed regularly, from the start. Then stopping the drug can be planned a long way ahead. The other response is to take seriously the advice that cognitive therapy should be the first line of treatment. If there is a chance that this will produce long term improvement then this would justify considerable investment; especially if the alternative is indefinite drug treatment.

There are problems for people who have made a good recovery but are still on medication. They may well want to stop the drug, but be worried about likely consequences. The trouble is that if you have been on a significant dose of an antipsychotic for many years, and you then stop it, there is a real risk that you will have a psychotic episode, even if you have been well for years. The only advice seems to be to choose a time when you are not under particular stress and reduce the dose of the drug gradually over many months. If you then start to experience psychotic symptoms, rather than discontinuation symptoms, then you should go back on the drug.

Accounts from people who have made a good recovery include many who have concluded that they must never stop their medication. There is a significant group of people who have done very well with antipsychotic medication, but who become unwell again every time they try to live without it. They learn by trial and error that they need to stay on medication. They then have a problem because of the ideology in many mental health groups that taking medication is not a good thing. It is assumed that once you are feeling well you will come off the drugs. There are certainly people who need to stay on drugs on a long term basis, and it is unfortunate that certain groups sneer at this, implying that the only good recovery is the drug free one. The overselling of drug treatment, and the pressuring of all to take drugs, has contributed to widespread hostility to this form of treatment. It results in the group who have most to gain being uncomfortable continuing with treatment.

I have tried to give a balanced view on drugs. I think it is irresponsible to devalue the real benefits that many get from medication. I am advocating thoughtful and selective use of drugs. Many who make good recoveries manage their lives with little or no medication; or use it only at particular times. Others stay on medication for years, but are made to feel bad about this by people who disapprove of it. This goes back to my plea to take ideology out of the subject. The aim is for people to own their recovery, to take responsibility for it. It is difficult to do that if part of your programme is medication which you have always seen as alien and unwanted.

Philosophical after-thought

Man has evolved over millions of years. He has learnt to speak, to write, and to carry out scientific experiments. However the human brain is said to be the most complex structure in the universe, and how consciousness and free will are connected to it remains a mystery. Several different theories have been developed to explain how the mind and the brain are related, but none is satisfactory. The 'Mysterian' theory (McGinn 1991) appeals to those who dislike the arrogance of scientists and philosophers. These claim by convoluted arguments to have solved this ancient problem: for example the 'identity theorists' who say that the brain and states of mind are simply the same thing. It is not at all clear what this means, but we are meant to believe it, just because people say it is true. The Mysterians argue instead that the problem of consciousness is a mystery, it lies beyond human comprehension. We lack the right concepts; our concepts of mental and physical are simply too crude to give us insight into how mind and body are related. Consequently thinking on the subject goes on and on, round and round, without coming to any conclusion. Most philosophers and scientists hate this idea, but I like it. It leads on to speculations about our current thinking about drugs and how the brain works.

Drug treatment has a very long and interesting history. Drugs have been used to make people feel different since before civilisation, since people were living in caves. Now our researchers are not only trying to find new substances to make people feel better, they are also trying to explain what goes on in the brain. They have theories to account for conditions such as schizophrenia, theories based on the most up to date knowledge of brain function. Chemicals are identified which are thought to play a part, based on the fact that their level at critical places in the brain are disturbed, That is, levels of one or two chemicals, found somewhere within the most complex structure in the universe. The theories predict that if the levels of the aberrant chemicals can be corrected, then the disease will improve. The way to achieve this is to take the tablets, so that the drug enters all the cells throughout the body. In this way the most complex structure in the universe will be 'fine-tuned'.

I am a Mysterian when it comes to brain chemistry. I can accept that drugs can have non-specific effects, calming or alerting the brain. These may be very useful for people suffering from mental illness. What I can't believe is that we can know what is going on in the brain when someone has disturbing experiences; or that we can devise a pill that is relevant to that person's particular problem. I do not think those who recommend drug treatment, which I often do, need to be signed up to the programme of finding a physical basis for everything in the brain. It is much less contentious simply to be offering remedies which may or may not help. This uncoupling of the medical approach to relieving distress from fundamentalist materialism would help to make it more acceptable to many.

Chapter 13
THE HUMAN FACTOR

Therapy is the other main type of specific treatment for people with mental health problems. This used to be seen as something American or European, but it is now firmly established in the UK. Therapies come in all shapes and sizes from the long and expensive to the cheap and cheerful. It has become a large service industry, with training in therapy a significant part of higher education. The NHS used to be outside the therapy world, but now there is growing pressure for NHS mental health workers to train as therapists.

The question is therefore; if people want to recover, is therapy what they need? The theories behind the therapies make lots of claims, but are they justified? The alternative view is that therapies tap into something that is much more primitive and basic; that is the need to talk and be in touch with other people. The null hypothesis is that all therapies are more or less complicated ways of supplying this basic human need. They provide personal contact, highly focused attention, hope of improvement and a theory to make sense of what has happened. The fact that they are meeting basic needs would explain their popularity, and the rather odd finding that they all seem to produce fairly similar results.

The validation question

The question of whether psychotherapy is effective was keenly debated for many years. It was the front line in a battle between very different approaches to psychiatry. I mentioned that Sargant did not believe that psychoanalysis was effective, and it was the psychologist Hans Eysenck who produced research evidence to back this up. He used data from insurance

149

claims in America to show that a significant proportion of people who were off work because of psychiatric problems got better and were able to return to work, even without any treatment. By pooling together a number of studies he concluded that "67% of seriously ill neurotic patients recover within two years, even in the absence of formal psychotherapy." This he called "spontaneous recovery", and he used it as a baseline against which to measure any study that claimed that psychotherapy was effective. He then added together the findings of available studies of psychotherapy and found that in 5 studies of psychoanalysis, with 760 subjects 44% recovered, and in 19 studies of eclectic psychotherapy with 7293 subjects 64% recovered. His conclusion was "the more the psychotherapy, the smaller the recovery rate."

This was a very provocative argument, which did a lot to stimulate research into psychotherapy. Eysenck's first paper on this subject came out in 1952, and the argument went on for many years (Eysenck 1992) It turned out to be very difficult to do satisfactory research into psychotherapy. For research the cases and the treatment have to be standardised, yet in psychotherapy every patient has unique problems and the approach taken has to be adapted to suit the individual. It is also difficult to standardise outcome measures since most therapy aims to change attitudes and underlying feelings more than symptoms. Many experimental studies were carried out, often at great expense and over prolonged periods. When these were published they were always found to fall far short of what people like Eysenck would regard as adequate. When viewed from the sidelines the argument looked like a good illustration of Kuhn's separate paradigms theory. Great effort was going into the studies, but the results were not convincing anyone. Those in the psychotherapy camp saw each new study as further confirmation of the effectiveness of psychotherapy, those opposed to psychotherapy saw the exact opposite. By the 1980's there was a move to place greater reliance on meta-analyses, where large numbers of studies were grouped together to give average results. These seemed to convince the therapists that their case was finally home and dry, proved by all the complicated statistics. I think at that stage the opponents either lost interest in the argument, or died off. Certainly by that time therapy had become established in the culture of the country, and the validation question was no longer critical. Interestingly, also going back to Kuhn, its becoming established had nothing to do with the research effort.

Therapy

Therapy is now an established part of the UK landscape. The therapist has become a well known figure, like "the doctor" or "the accountant"; people think they know what a therapist is even if they have never met one. So what are some of the features of this institution?

1) A Formula: There are sessions, held on a regular basis, continuing for a certain time. Sessions are usually an hour, during which the client has the therapist's undivided attention. It is usual for the client to pay, though in some settings there the service may be free. There is much emphasis on confidentiality, and the focus is on the thoughts and feelings of the client, rather than their practical life problems.

2) A set of beliefs: Therapists are trained in an approach which gives them a way to understand their clients' problems. The models used are extraordinarily varied. Any organised way of understanding people, the world and life in general can become the basis of a form of therapy. The model gives the therapist confidence to be able to offer to help. To a variable extent the clients become aware of, and benefit from learning to apply the model to themselves.

3) A controlled situation: Therapists undertake to help and not to harm their clients. It is accepted that there should be close and intimate discussion within a safe setting. There are procedures for investigating and stopping rogue therapists. The safety of the situation is important for people who are at their most vulnerable when seeking help.

4) A socially acceptable option: Therapy has less stigma than most other forms of mental health care. Having therapy is seen in some circles as a reasonable thing to do, even quite interesting; much more acceptable than going to a psychiatric clinic.

Therapy has now achieved the status of a social institution. It provides a livelihood for a large group of people, and is accepted as the right way to deal with emotional problems – however defined. The days of empirical challenge are passed, so that it is no longer polite to ask whether or not psychotherapy is effective. This leads to a confidence, indeed arrogance, similar to that of the advocates of drug treatment. It tends to be assumed that the way therapy is delivered, the formula, has some established validity, that it is fixed in stone. As with drugs, the pressure groups that support therapy make exaggerated claims and do not like critical comment.

An alternative view is that therapy is a social institution which derives its strength from the real need that people have for human support and contact when dealing with personal problems. It works in so far as it meets this need, but has problems and limitations of its own.

Limits and criticisms of therapy

1) Not for all. Therapy is rarely able to help people who are going through a severe crisis, or suffering from a acute psychotic disorder. The formality of therapy requires that people are managing their lives reasonably well – so that they can attend regular sessions and cope in between. Because of the social acceptability of therapy, people often seek it when what they really need is acute psychiatric help.

2) Cultural style. Therapy tends to incorporate a certain liberal white middle-class view of the world, and not everyone is comfortable with this. It also has an implicit message that the right way to be is direct and open, showing your feelings and saying what you think. Those whose temperaments are very different from this can find it difficult.

3) Inbuilt conservatism. The emphasis of therapy is on thoughts and feelings rather than reality. Most people who have serious mental health problems are struggling with major problems in their life. They may be isolated, poor, unemployed or in difficult relationships. They may also have suffered from abuse in the past. The strategy of therapy is to deal with these problems in the consulting room, by changing how the person is thinking about them and reacting to them. To many this can seem like a subtle way of blaming the

person for their suffering. The message is that it is not the world that causes the trouble, but the person's neurotic reaction. To quote Pilgrim(1992)

"Psychoanalysis and humanistic psychology are prone to particular forms of reductionism in their conception of the human condition. This leads to their being conservative-by-default in that they frame socially derived forms of oppression as individual problems."

This is a radical argument which impresses some people. It is certainly the case that some people are temperamentally unsuited to therapy.

Psychotherapy is a specific form of treatment that many find helpful. It is claimed that by working in a particular way, and following a prescribed course, it is possible to help people. Therapists say that they can understand the cause of the person's problems, and help to resolve them by approaching them in a particular way. Even if one does not believe the specific claims that are made, therapy should deliver many of the vital non-specific benefits that people need. This will be true as long as the therapist is sensitive and considerate, and is not following some unhelpful or even harmful therapeutic approach. In other words therapy can be very helpful when it is good, but harmful when it is bad. There is nothing in the formula which guarantees anything. The client therefore needs to monitor progress. The relationship that develops is vital and if it is not good, then it will not be helpful. The personality and style of the therapist may be more important than the brand of therapy that they are following.

Cognitive Behaviour Therapy (CBT)

(CBT) is a sort of therapy, but it has evolved a bit further. It is less intellectual and passive than traditional therapy, and appeals to a wider group of people. It has become the most widely used therapy in the NHS. It developed from cognitive therapy, which was started in the USA by Aaron Beck as a treatment for depression, and has now been adapted for most kinds of problem including psychosis. It incorporates many non-specific benefits that were neglected in more traditional therapy. CBT is targeted at particular problems that are identified by the client. Then client and therapist work together to come up with solutions. There is a focus on studying the clients' thoughts and behaviour, often by some sort of recording or self-observation that is then used in planning intervention. Clients are helped to reflect on their own thoughts, assess their validity and if necessary change them. The whole process is very much out in the open, so that studying and learning are part of the process. Homework assignments are used to carry what has been learnt into the client's daily life. The learning part of CBT helps to dispel some of the mystification that can surround psychiatric treatment.

CBT can be used with any mental health problem; it provides a basic approach that can be adapted. Its strength is that it is open and explicit, and can utilise any new findings of psychological study as they become available. It can make use of studies of positive psychology and happiness, as these can help generate ideas about how people can restructure their lives. It fits in well with recovery models, being eclectic, and designed to fit around the clients' needs. The rise of CBT in popularity is a sign of the sea change that this book is all about.

Survival stories

Many of those who have recovered stress the importance of particular people in their struggle for recovery. These may be professionals, they are often friends or other people who are going through similar experiences. Coleman (1999) talks of people who were his "navigators back to normality". Others have spoken of the importance of finding a mentor. In most stories there is someone, often many people.

How can one find a mentor, or 'navigator'? And what are their characteristics? They must make contact at a personal level. It may be someone who has been through similar experiences, or at least knows what is going on. There has to be some kind of positive relationship. This simple ingredient is the most important, and the most difficult to define. How can positive, helpful relationships be set-up, organised, part of a health care system? That is the big question.

It might be that there is nothing here that a professional can do that a good sensible and well informed friend could not do. The trouble is that when it really counts most people do not have such a friend available. There are also real barriers to turning to those around you. It is not easy to talk openly about personal problems if you are not used to doing this and it is also true that not everyone is a good listener. It is easy to get it wrong; to be too quick to reassure or offer advice, or too slow to show that you understand. If someone takes the risk of confiding in another and then finds that they are not understood, or not taken seriously, this is a major setback. Unfortunately this happens with professionals as well as friends. Professionals have a bad reputation for listening and being understanding. There is an ingrained bossiness that is endemic in government services the world over. It is seen as a priority to tell people things and explain (called 'educating the public') rather than listening. There are systems that have to be followed, so that if people say what they would like, or how they would like things to be done, they have to be told that it is not possible. The mental health services struggle against this, and one might think that if there was anywhere that people could be heard it would be there. But systems, organisations and institutions are intimidating at the best of times. When you work in psychiatric hospitals you become used to it, hardened. To patients it can be very frightening, which explains why it is not always easy to find someone in whom to confide.

The person who is chosen as a confidant is often the least threatening person. So it may not be the psychiatrist, who might get you sectioned if you say the wrong thing, or the nurse who might say you are not ready to go home, but the ward cleaner who is easier to talk to. Also the cleaner who is struggling on a low wage with an unpopular job may have more immediate rapport with the patient on the ward.

A confidant turns out to be one of the surest aids to recovery but is difficult to arrange. In professional services people work in teams and the importance of personal contact can be overlooked. It is part of the culture that since it is treatment that gets you better, it doesn't matter who administers it. Patients who make a fuss and demand to stay in touch with a particular person are seen as demanding or manipulative. There are good reasons for team working and for patients not becoming too dependent on one person, but these have to be balanced with the need for meaningful contact.

In the past I have often struggled to find a professional who can offer a supportive relationship to someone going through a crisis; somehow providing this doesn't seem to be in anybody's job description. What the person needs is someone to stick with them. I have been lucky to work in teams with people who could do this – but their ability to do it depended more on their personality and values rather than any special training. Indeed, the more highly trained a person becomes the less freedom of action they seem to have. Instead there would be questions about "What sort of therapy" and "Are they really motivated?" This is an example of my main thesis – that the powerful and effective benefits of non-specific measures are denied people because of the focus on specific treatments.

Fortunately new services such as Crisis Teams and Home Treatment are explicitly recognising the need to support people through periods of crisis. However such teams operate with strict referral criteria, to stop them being overwhelmed. Their work tends to be time limited, certainly not extending to the long periods during which people need help. It will still be important to put someone in touch with a good person who can stand by them in a bad time – as that is precisely what is needed. I fear that as the new services become more sophisticated and professional all the effort will go into specific interventions and again there will be a reluctance to take people on and stick with them.

Positive end point

One answer to criticisms of therapy is that fortunately most therapists do not do what they say they do. They are in fact caring, kind, supportive people who do more for their clients than their textbooks say they should. Similarly one finds that community psychiatric nurses do not maintain a rigid distance from their patients, but actually befriend them. People are taught a lot about maintaining their professional role, and yet once they have mastered this, they learn to express their own personality in their work. They are not faceless employees of the state, but people with needs of their own trying to make their way in an uncertain world.

CBT is very acceptable to most people, and becoming more widely available; but it is not a panacea. It will help some people, but not others. The importance of relationships is increasingly recognised and is one of the main features of Home Treatment and Assertive Outreach Teams. Newer types of mental health worker such as community care workers now deliberately befriend their clients. Befriending enables the worker to support someone in a wide range of activities. They can be involved in doing things rather than just talking. This is very different from the model of therapy. Instead of working to correct some hypothetical disorder in thinking, befriending seeks to help someone maximise opportunities for recovery - wherever they are.

Chapter 14
SURVIVAL OF THE PERSONAL LIFE

Personal recovery involves much more than losing symptoms. It involves becoming a person again, regaining a personal life that has some value and meaning. This aspect of recovery has been neglected in British psychiatry. In America apparently, things are very different; their books on mental health have a lot to say about spirituality. One popular self help book for people suffering from depression says "Almost all our patients describe themselves as spiritual persons," and "for most of us, spirituality is at the core of our being."(Wright & Basco 2002) This is not the way that most people in the UK talk about themselves: here the word "spirituality" will set a lot of people's teeth on edge. Yet this area is just as important over here.

Aspects of the person extend beyond the narrow confines of their immediate needs and survival to include interests, involvements and commitment to others. The spiritual includes our understanding of ourselves and our place in the world. It goes beyond intellectual understanding to our sense of being in the world, grounded in it and belonging to it. The world and our life can have a meaning in which we are aware of being connected to our history, our present and our future. The sense of belonging is enhanced by contact with other people; with the natural world and with the products of our culture. From the groundedness that people feel, they derive inner strength; a sense of optimism and of being in control. The ability to accept others and to behave in an altruistic way serves to support people's connectedness to the human race. All these facets of life are underpinned for many by the teachings and traditions of their religion. What they have come to believe from an early age confirms their position in the world.

Being involved with a religious group may be a key part of this, but in our secular society there are many other types of involvement that can give meaning to people's lives. Some of these involve a measure of altruism, but many people derive most of their sense of purpose from their involvement with their immediate friends and family. This meaningfulness of life is the easiest thing to take for granted. It is only when the background of people and activity stops that it becomes apparent that it supplied a vital ingredient to life.

I am particularly interested in the spiritual life of the unspiritual; the religion of the religionless. There is a background of shared experience, participation and history that enables people to tolerate their lives. It is part of a narrative account that they have constructed over the years, often from the most unpromising material. This works as long as it works, but it can be swept aside by mental illness. This fabric may seem very solid and secure, and may never have been appreciated as the background to someone's life. The positive feeling towards one's own life is the easiest thing to take for granted. It can be lost quickly when someone loses all sense of their own worth. It can also be shattered when key parts of the framework, such as family, or occupation or good health are lost.

The person who recovers faces the problem of reconstructing some vision beyond the immediate present. Hopes may have gone as well as reasons to carry on. Then there is the loss of warm feelings for what was previously special. Activities stop, interests are lost, people excluded. Over a period of time the ingredients of the personal life are scattered on the winds. I am used to meeting people at the stage when these have all gone and to quote from the poem 'Shadows' by D.H.Lawrence: their "life is only the leavings of a life." At that point, all professional concern may be focused on risk management, getting the medication right, and implementing the Mental Health Act. The person may be confined in a fairly bleak ward environment and totally disengaged from what is happening to them. Someone encountered in such a setting can easily be seen as less than a person, and they may be treated accordingly.

The reductionism of naïve psychiatry does not concern itself with all this. It is an assumption of the scientific approach that anything that affects a person will be covered by medicine and psychology. If spiritual matters are seen as just an expression of people's psychology and their state of health, then psychology and health are all that one needs to study. If recovery was just the restoration of health to what it was before, this would be possible. The naïve idea persists that once there is remission of symptoms all will return to normal. The spiritual aspect of life tends to be left out of discussions of psychiatry, except in the writings of those who identify themselves as practising Christians. This can lead to the idea that spiritual issues are something optional, only relevant to those who subscribe to one of the established religions. This is how it tends to be in psychiatric hospitals, where anything spiritual is seen as the province of the hospital chaplain. So, if people start talking about God we send for the chaplain, and if they don't, the area gets ignored.

As people emerge from periods of mental turmoil their spiritual life is often barren and empty. The experiences of psychosis may have fragmented their sense of identity and inner strength. They may have become disconnected from the life that was planned, and the person they thought they were becoming. Meaninglessness is a common feeling when people are depressed, and in the post - psychotic state. The whole world can appear flat - lacking purpose and direction.

So how can the spirit recover? It is an embarrassingly 'New Age' sort of question for a psychiatrist to try to answer. It is clear that it is not more treatment that is needed. It is rather that whatever is done needs to help, encourage and support the efforts of the individual to rebuild their personal life. One way to keep the focus on the individual is to have a 'Personal Recovery Plan' (Coleman 1999). This will list the person's aims and aspirations, and help to make sure that any interventions are consistent with these.

Many of the slightly surprising things that people report as having helped them during recovery involve some reconnection with a continuing inner life. Contact with nature, and being in beautiful surroundings is often mentioned by people as important. This may not be on any elevated or grand scale, but simply some encounter that has occurred. It may link back to old memories of being close to the natural world in the past - maybe in childhood. Or it may be a new experience. It might be working in the garden, in the drizzle in February. It might be sitting in the afternoon in the hospital grounds. People who are recovering may get back in touch with sources of comfort that they have known in the past. Or they may, for the first time, make real connections with sources of strength outside themselves. This is one area where people describe themselves coming out of mental illness with enhanced awareness and sensitivity.

Interesting discussions have taken place over the closure of old, out of date hospitals. In one place, all the plans were made for a new unit that would be better in every way. It was going to be modern and comfortable, with every patient having their own room. Planners were then surprised to find that the only group opposing the move was the group of users of the service. They spoke lyrically of the value they attached to the lovely grounds of the old hospital that would now be lost. Modern hospitals are on small sites, near the town centre. There is no pleasure in walking around them. The move went ahead, and the beautiful grounds were lost. The grounds were an asset whose value was unquantifiable.

Another experience that may help restore the spirit is being useful and helpful to others. Such a way of relating to others may remind the person of goals and aspirations from the past, or may be a new experience. There are many instances where someone in hospital takes on a role helping someone else, and in the process derives benefit for his or her self. This kind of thing can be encouraged and supported.

Being able to withdraw, and spend time alone, is reported as helping recovery. For one person this involved meditation in the hospital gym. It is surprising how many non-believers talk of the powerful effect of visiting sacred sites of various kinds. They are places of peace and contemplation. Many things are remarked on as having helped, having been uplifting. They may take a person slightly outside his or her self. They may interrupt a persistent and depressing line of thought. These are the chance occurrences; the improbable meeting that sets in motion a completely different life: the backward glance as someone walks away after everything has gone wrong, and they see for the first time that it is different. Nobody can plan or arrange it but such things can help restore the spirit.

When people talk of how they would like to be helped through a crisis, they often describe something that sounds like a monastery or a retreat. It should be quiet and peaceful. There should be unobtrusive but helpful people around. There should be venerable buildings, preferably set in countryside, with beautiful trees. They picture themselves being able to sleep, take exercise and talk things over - if they want to. This fantasy has often been described to me and it is certainly one that I share. Occasionally I have been able to introduce someone to a place that bore some resemblance to this. There are places where people can go on retreat, but these are nearly all aimed at those who are members of religious groups. There is a lack of suitable places for the non-religious majority. So I have had to disappoint most people and admit them to an ordinary acute in-patient unit. Such units differ from the fantasy in every way. The buildings are not uplifting but noisy and crowded, and at times dangerous. Staying in such places is not usually under the individual's control, but in the hands of professionals. They are particularly hard on the spirit. It is difficult in such a place to raise one's eyes beyond the present. So how can this aspect of people's lives be nourished in such adverse circumstances?

1) Atmosphere

This may be the most important feature of any psychiatric unit, but is also the most difficult to define. A favourable atmosphere will help people. They will feel that they are being treated with respect, as individuals whose personal situation is taken into account. In a large bureaucratic organisation like the NHS it is a struggle to achieve this. There will always be regulations to follow and forms to be filled in. It is up to the people in charge of a unit to insist that the organisation is there for the patients, and not the other way round. They have to protect the patients from unnecessary bureaucracy.

People need peace and security, both of which are difficult to find on an acute ward. I know that after working on psychiatric wards for many years I am now used to some very bad things – and I don't have to stay for more than a few hours. There are still wards where patients are not safe because they have to share facilities with people who are restless and disinhibited. The staff may decide that a situation is safe, and therefore tolerable, but this may underestimate the emotional impact of witnessing someone going through a very disturbed episode. Too often there is just not enough space

- so unsuited groups of patients are put together. This creates a strong argument for Home Treatment, but this is not an option for all.

2) Respect

Personal contact between patients and staff is vitally important. This is not a question of staff being therapists, or experts in specific interventions, though it will help the ward to have staff with special training. It is about basic human contact for people who are in a state of some turmoil – frightened, confused, angry, despairing, etc. I have worked on wards where everyone was given time, supported, listened to, treated with respect and made to feel that they were worthy of being helped. I have also been in places where not one of these common courtesies was observed. Without this level of care, the experience of being in hospital can be very harmful. People get worse rather than better. My main point is that it is the non-specific aspects of care which set the tone of a ward, and determine whether or not it is a helpful place to be.

3) Home treatment

Home treatment is preferred by many people and their families. Even though it puts a strain on the family, that is often less than the strain of having someone in hospital. It is easier for people to hold onto their life when they are unwell, and regain it as they get better if they don't have to come into hospital. It also helps people stay in charge of running their own affairs. There is less disruption to the contacts and involvements that make up personal life. But like everything, it is not a panacea, and many situations arise where hospital is still needed. The option of using home treatment to reduce the amount of time spent in hospital is then useful.

4) Developing understanding

Making sense of what has happened is a major task for someone going through a mental health crisis. This is contentious, as there are so many ways of explaining things. Because so many different theoretical frameworks are used, people are told many different things and are often confused.

Since diagnosis is such a widely used way of describing what is wrong with people, it is only fair to tell them what their diagnosis is. It is then very necessary to explain the limits of the diagnostic process and remove any misconceptions. If someone learns that their diagnosis is schizophrenia, they may be very alarmed, and background information about what such a diagnosis might mean is essential. Some other diagnoses can be more obviously helpful. If a woman develops post-natal depression, she is often unaware of what has happened. Instead she may conclude that she is a bad person and a hopeless mother, and that everyone would be better off if she were not around. The idea that she has developed a well understood reaction to having a baby can be positive and helpful. This is true in many types of depression. To an outsider it is obvious that something is very wrong, but the person concerned may dismiss this, saying that they have always been like this. The thoughts that assail them are not new thoughts, they are the same negative thoughts that the person has had all their life. The difference now is that the person is no longer able to put them on one side, but is overwhelmed by them. The idea that they may be depressed is often dismissed.

Most clinicians regard diagnosis as of limited importance, and place more importance on the clinical formulation. This summarises the person's current problems, lists the factors that have contributed, and then reviews what can be done to improve things. It may be quite a long statement, describing in narrative form the development of the problems. It can be quite a revelation for someone to read their formulation; altogether more helpful than just hearing the diagnosis. It is proof that the person has been listened to carefully, and it may be the first time that they have seen a clear and meaningful account of how they got into their difficulties. One of the first to use written formulations as a therapeutic tool was Dr Anthony Ryle, the originator of Cognitive Analytical Therapy (CAT, Ryle 1995). CAT is a form of brief, focused analytical psychotherapy, designed to be simpler and more transparent than older analytical therapies. Therapist and client work together on a written formulation offering an explanation for the problem being addressed and proposed strategies for dealing with it. The client then has a copy of the formulation, and the therapy only goes ahead once it has been agreed and any necessary changes made. This is a very long way from the old wall of silence that prevailed in Freudian therapy.

The same kind of overt formulation is now suggested for all mental health work. There are care plans for all patients, and gradually habits of secrecy are being swept away. A care plan is an agreement to provide someone with a certain level of care; it is about service provision. A formulation is much more personal; it is an explanation which is to be the basis of intervention. It can also be the basis of personal understanding. The models used to provide the explanation will depend on the orientation of the person who wrote it. However if a formulation is to be helpful it needs to include the framework of understanding that is used by the patient. One universal framework is the life history. If people can see things as arising from the narrative of their own life, that is likely to be meaningful. Plotting life events, and showing how these contribute to emotional changes is a basic explanatory tool, first developed by Adolph Meyer (Gelder 1991).

5) Protection

Mental health workers should be strictly non-partisan, upholding the law, but not pushing one view rather than another. We have to be able to let people make their own lives, including their own mistakes. However, there are times when we have to come off the fence. If there is a common ideology to mental health work it is to do with the value of the individual. There are times when we have to protect those who come to see us. There may be parents, spouses or children who are abusing them. There may be employers who want us to help them against the wishes of our patients. There may be people who have nobody and nothing. It is then important to remember that we work for our patients, and that although there is a publicly funded health service, this is not a police state.

6) Specific interventions

Activity and involvement are important for recovery, yet they are sadly lacking in hospitals, where boredom and inactivity are big problems. Being in a psychiatric hospital is desperately boring. If people have difficulty motivating themselves, this is made much worse by being in a place where there is nothing to do. There are times when a person does not want to do anything, and rest and inactivity serve a purpose, but this is limited. The traditional medical response is to recommend "occupational therapy". For some this provides valuable relief from inactivity, and helps re-engagement, for others it is childish and demeaning. Much will depend on the attitude of the occupational therapist, and what they are trying to achieve. I have worked with some very skilled and sensitive occupational therapists, able to help people find some meaningful activity that has been decisive in getting them going again after prolonged periods of inactivity. I have also seen "doing O.T." being prescribed without any reference to the individual's situation, and being a meaningless exercise.

There are often arguments about whether providing activity is in itself useful for people, or whether it has to be in some way therapeutic or educational. I am convinced that it is the activity that matters, but it may be essential to have help and encouragement in order to get started. The art lies in helping someone to become involved, someone who may find participation very difficult. A major advantage of activity is that it provides a good setting in which people can start to be with other people. There are useful analogies here to people getting over physical injuries. There was a time when long periods of bed rest were recommended, but these are now seen as entirely unhelpful. People are made to get out of bed practically as soon as they can stand up. We need the same attitude in mental health, getting people doing things as soon as possible; not waiting until they are better. The longer they wait, the worse it will be.

Creative activities are often used in hospitals and many have found them helpful. There are chances for stimulating and inspiring work. However it can be a bit like school – where some children are inspired, but many are bored and irritated. Art therapy can be a bit off-putting if there is too much emphasis on interpreting what people are doing, the emphasis needs to be on the art, not the therapy. The main thing is for people to be able to create and express themselves. Studios are now being established – for example at 'Studio Upstairs' - where people can continue with their artistic work over long periods as part of their personal recovery process.

7) Alternative approaches

Alternative medicine derives much of its appeal from being linked to non-reductive, unorthodox theories. It links recovery to aspects of life that many people think are important. The fact that some doctors say that these approaches are based on nonsensical theories will confirm for those who reject the reductive worldview that they must be on to something. The concepts behind many alternative treatments are alien, or at least new to western culture. This enhances their credibility for some people, and hence their effectiveness. The value of placebo treatments depends on people believing in them, so any safe procedure in which people believe is likely to do them good. The word 'placebo' is an obvious put-down. What is involved are traditional ways of helping people which do not use toxic chemicals.

The other key element is the people involved. Alternative treatments are often given by individuals who are struggling to work on their own and are highly motivated to provide a good service. There is emphasis on the individual, with a personal service being provided. This supplies many of ingredients of service in which the NHS fails.

8) Residential options

The role of residential placements in fostering recovery is a vast subject which could fill a book of its own. It has a long history, including such notables as Joseph Conolly and non-restraint and also the Moral Treatment Movement. It is generally accepted that during the nineteenth century, as the institutions became bigger, they lost their aspiration to help people to recover. They became more like warehouses for the mentally ill from which people had to escape if they were to recover. Psychiatric hospitals have remained a bit like this - places that contain people, try to keep them safe and bring their severe symptoms under control.

The old long stay wards of hospitals have closed and their patients have moved on. Some went to small houses in the community where great efforts were made to help them to regain a life for themselves after years away. Others ended up becoming isolated, and having little help or support.

The idea that being in hospital can be helpful in itself has faded, as the wards have become more acute and busy. This does not mean that efforts are not made to make staying in hospital helpful, but it is an uphill struggle, and the conclusion must be that hospital is not a place to stay any longer than is absolutely necessary.

There remain places where Therapeutic Communities have been established, and continue to flourish. These have always been interesting, different places, often attracting colourful characters as staff members and clients. Some are set up to treat people with a particular type of problem, using a specialised form of group therapy. There are many places that take people with drug and alcohol problems, and there are also communities aimed at people suffering from personality disorders. In addition to these there is a large number of projects that take people with more varied problems. Most of these are small organisations which work outside the statutory services. Their independent status helps to add to their interest and mystique. To find and be accepted by one of these places is in itself an achievement, and possibly a secret of their success. The motivation that can get you there, should also help you to benefit from being there.

Common features of the therapeutic communities are:

Small size

Living together, expected to become a social group.

Shared activities

Expectations of active participation

Lengthy stays – at least several months.

Communities vary according to the therapeutic model they use. Some are strongly influenced by group therapy ideas, others less so. Some are very prescriptive, such as those for substance users which require all drugs and medications to be stopped before people enter, with immediate discharge for anyone taking any substances.

These places can be helpful experiences for the right people at the right time. It is necessary to be ready for the place when you go there, ready to start to recover. There are certainly people with acute problems who will not have reached that point. They are just trying to survive, to hang on. There is a 'readiness for change', which is needed. More could be learnt about this. It seems to involve some degree of acceptance of what has happened to you, and enough pain from it to want to change. There also needs to be some hope, something positive, some attraction to this strange community. This is part of the reason why communities do not make it too easy for people to join, they have to work at it a bit. This is very different from the ethos of the acute ward to which people can be admitted when they have a positive motivation not to be there. It is a clear illustration of the different tasks that arise at different stages in the recovery process, and of how the wards are not primarily aimed at recovery.

Chapter 15

REGAINING CONTROL

The psychiatrist's curse

The use of legal powers under the Mental Health Act to detain and treat people is what separates psychiatrists from the rest; from their colleagues and the rest of humanity. There are many jokes about the psychiatrist being different, a bit frightening; someone who can take away your freedom. It is a unique power given to psychiatrists, and it contributes a lot to the negative reactions to psychiatry. It may be a joke for one's colleagues, but it is a serious matter for one's patients. People try to find ways round the problem, some of them positive and helpful, others evasive or plain dishonest. However it is something that has to be faced, as treating people against their wishes is central to psychiatry.

In most in-patient units it is only a minority of patients who are detained under the Mental Health Act. In many places it is less than 25%, though in some inner city areas this percentage may be much higher. It might be argued that this indicates that compulsion is affecting only a minority of service users. However when I looked at this more closely, I found that for nearly all patients compulsion is a major issue. If 25% of patients are currently detained under the Mental Health Act, then at least an equal number has been detained at some time in the past. Then there will be a similar number where active discussions have gone on in the staff group about whether or not the person should be detained. With some of these it may have been decided that if that person decides to leave the ward, they should be assessed with a view to detaining them. I have found that in 75% or more of in-patients, detention, or the possibility of it plays a major part in the management of care.

The issue is not an easy one for professionals. This figure of 75% means that in all these cases the professionals know that they can be judged to be negligent if they fail to use the powers available to them. The psychological effects of this are profound on both sides. The effects have become more intense in recent years due to high profile cases where professionals have been blamed for failing to prevent disasters. The message that has come from such cases is that members of staff are responsible for the outcome; - that if only they did their jobs properly, tragedies would not happen. Doing the job properly involves using the full powers of any available legislation, and imposing detention in hospital and drug treatment to the fullest extent allowed by the law.

So the psychiatrist's curse remains, and is as powerful now as it has ever been. It is no answer to imply that it is simply wrong to detain anyone: it is easy to say that, but not responsible or helpful. These powers are not just an option that can be invoked in exceptional circumstances. They need to be considered in the management of each patient. It is better to start a discussion about the importance of autonomy for recovery by recognising that we in the mental health services are in a business that has enormous powers to restrict autonomy. It is important to accept just how big a problem this is. The question, then, is how can the practice of psychiatry change so that less use is made of compulsion, and when this is used, how can its negative effects be reduced?

Promoting autonomy

Autonomy is vital for recovery - but the traditions and culture of psychiatry work against it. This means that unless positive action is taken, this vital ingredient in recovery is actively suppressed by the very system that is supposed to be fostering it.
Patients have to assert themselves against a system that seeks to keep them safe by controlling them.
This is not an area where there is logical consistency, or where there are neat logical answers to the problems. Confusions in the mental health field reflect those in wider society. There are a series of opposing arguments, so the outcomes can not be laid down in advance. For example:

Keep people safe, stop them coming to harm: versus let them be autonomous and make their own decisions.

People want help and advice, versus they want to be able to decide their own future

Society must be protected from mad people: versus vulnerable people must be protected from society

A wide range of treatment options should be available, versus everything must be regulated.

It is a mistake to pretend that it is either the individual or society that is right. It is an ancient and continuing struggle. To take an extreme position gives one the pleasure of certainty, but it does not work when one is called to help someone in an emergency. One suspects that those who make sweeping statements to resolve this issue at a stroke have never had day to day responsibilities in the field of acute psychiatry.

At any one time several different social movements are under way. It may be satisfying to blame everything on 'The Government' for not being consistent, but the world is not a consistent place. There is a movement to improve the lot of people who are disadvantaged by reason of mental illness which has been going on since the nineteenth century. I have seen dramatic improvements over the past thirty five years. There is still a long way to go, and the Recovery Movement marks a new stage in this. There are also public concerns about what happens to people with mental health problems if they are left too much to their own devices. There is concern that some of them harm others, some commit suicide, and many end up in prison. There is now a new bout of public debate about whether it would be better if laws controlling people with mental disorders could be more restrictive. One strong argument against new laws is that new services to deliver better support to people outside hospital have only started operating in the past few years, so it is too soon to see whether new laws are needed.

Reducing the need for compulsion

There is a tendency to play down the impact of compulsion on patients; like the bad conditions on the wards, compulsion is something that professionals get hardened to. This reduces the importance given to steps aimed at reducing that impact. If compulsion is a big and difficult issue then there are many things that can be done, and these concern the non-specific aspects of care rather than any treatment.

Compulsory treatment may be avoidable by:

1) Personal contacts

If someone who is in a crisis is seen by people who know them it is far more likely that a non-compulsory option will be found. This simple common-sense measure is often ignored by services. The result is that what might have been a minor health review turns into a major incident - literally - with police, ambulances sirens etc. in attendance.

2) Preferred options

If people can say how they want to be treated in a crisis, and these requests are available, then compulsion may be avoided. To go into a local ward, or a ward where they got on well with the staff rather than one where they did not, may be what is required. The professional response to this may be: "Who is in charge here? Is this person going to tell us how they should be treated?" These issues, so costly in personal, professional and financial terms are still often decided on the basis of such low sentiments. Professionals find it difficult to give people what they want, especially if they are difficult and demanding. There remains a culture of bossiness. This can be overcome by good people putting such attitudes behind them, and doing their best to find a solution. In the last resort, it is simple, good, human qualities that can achieve a good result. Most who go to work in mental health possess these qualities, so the question is how can organisations bring this out and not suppress it? Challenging bossiness in public facilities could be a lifetime's work.

3) Alternatives to admission

Home Treatment and Crisis Teams will often be acceptable to

someone who would otherwise be admitted to hospital under the Mental Health Act. They specialise in fitting in with people while making sure the person receives a safe level of care, which may well include medication. I have found that people often refuse medication because it is one of the few areas of their life where they can still exercise some control. If every effort is made to fit in with someone's request to be treated at home, they are less likely to refuse medication out of hand. There are also other places that someone might go apart from a hospital. This could be the house of a friend or member of the family. Non-hospital 'safe houses' have their advocates, but I have no experience of these.

Reducing the negative effect of compulsion

1) Personal contacts

The mental health system can be frightening and Kafkaesque. The experience of being on an acute ward can result in traumatic stress. It is important that the key players keep in close contact throughout an admission. This is not a complicated idea, but it often fails to happen. It is especially important if someone has to move between different wards during their time in hospital.

2) Information

It should be possible to make a person aware of how and why decisions are being made. The psychiatrist who is the Responsible Medical Officer (RMO) needs to spend time discussing the legal predicament that binds him or her to the patient. The RMO has considerable freedom about how to use their compulsory powers, and there is much room for dialogue and negotiation. People who are detained can benefit from having an advocate, to talk to, and to talk on their behalf. Such a person can assist in discussions with a RMO. A written statement of the legal position, and the reasons for it can be helpful. All these things are costly and time consuming. They will not be likely to be available in services that are short of money.

3) Appeals

The appeal process requires the RMO to come up with clear plans for future care. The discussions to produce a plan will often remove the need for a hearing. If there is an irreconcilable difference of opinion, then a hearing can help to generate new options by opening it up to a wider group.

4) Restoring autonomy

This needs to begin straight away. It is not easy to maintain a regime that can impose restrictions when people are admitted to hospital, and then start to give back the power to make decisions almost straight away. Psychiatrists have personality traits which mean that they tend to adopt a particular style in dealing with people. Some are authoritarian; comfortable giving instructions and telling people what to do. Others are liberal and easy going, finding it difficult to impose their will on others and finding it easier to give people what they want. What is required is that each psychiatrist has to learn to play each role and to be able to switch quickly from one to the other.

5) Advance directives

Psychiatric advance directives are one way that patients can feel less helpless about the treatment that they receive when they are detained under the Mental Health Act. These can be used by people who have recurrent episodes during which they lose the capacity to make decisions for themselves. They can specify in advance how they want to be treated if they suffer from a relapse. This can be discussed with the team; a process involving the person in areas of their care from which they are usually excluded. The patient is not then relying on the psychiatrist making decisions on his or her behalf.

These ideas are difficult for professionals. An advance directive may specify a plan that is difficult to carry out, or is not expected to produce rapid improvement. Surely in that case it can be overruled? These are early days for advance directives in mental health, but the limited experience I have of them leads me to think they may bring benefits over the longer period. The use of an advance directive begins a process of involving the person in their own treatment decisions. The first directive that is made may not be ideal but it can then be amended in the light of experience. After all, the first treatment plan put forward by the doctor may also not work. This introduces a whole new area of feed-back for the person. An area of their life that was previously under strict medical control is now something that they can influence. The learning process also goes the other way - in that the psychiatrist can develop a better understanding of the real priorities for the patient. I spent years talking to patients about the overriding importance of preventing relapses at any cost - only to find in the end that few shared this perspective. If the cost of preventing a relapse was to take drugs that turned you into a zombie, made you put on two stone in weight and interfered with your sex life, then it was clearly too high a cost.

User empowerment

"User empowerment" has become a popular idea with service planners, but too often it is seen as just one more thing that you can 'do' to people. The idea that users need this thing called "empowerment", leads to the paradoxical suggestion that it can be provided in some special form of therapy. The paradox in such an idea is that the more you do to people, the less chance they have of taking control of their own lives. You can't really empower people; they have to do this for themselves.

The law is used not just to keep people safe during acute crises, but also to enforce a long-term treatment plan. Such enforcement has only been possible up to now for patients who were detained in hospital. However, plans for reform of the law now envisage continuing treatment against people's wishes over prolonged periods. The issue of compulsory treatment outside hospital has been debated for a long time. It would be a very major extension of state control.

I know well the sort of people for whom the new arrangements are thought necessary and justified. There have been times when I have said 'if only' a certain person could be made to stay on their medication, then they would remain well. Fifteen years ago I would have supported the idea of extending compulsory treatment. Now, after more experience working with better services outside hospital, I am opposed to it. I see it as perpetuating the kinds of services that produce chronic long-term patients, who lead stable but very limited lives.

Linda

Linda was one such person. When I met her she had already spent many years going in and out of hospitals. She suffered from recurring bouts of mania, during which she would become disinhibited in her behaviour and preoccupied with religious delusions, including the idea that her daughter was the Virgin Mary. In her disturbed state she would wander the streets, often stopping passers by to preach the gospel, or to berate them for their sins. On several occasions she was assaulted by people she confronted in this way. Usually Linda had an infectious warmth, but as she built up to one of her 'episodes', she would develop a hard, critical, paranoid edge. On a number of occasions I had to visit her in police cells and arrange her admission to hospital under the Mental Health Act. Such episodes were difficult, with Linda being very angry and threatening. She would accuse me of letting her down, and complain that all the drugs she had been given were poisoning her. She would vow never to speak to me again, and demand to see another psychiatrist. Then in hospital Linda would gradually settle down. She would be started on medication, and would fairly quickly get used to the familiar routine of the ward. Once we got to that stage Linda would be charming again, and would soon be persuading me that she was well enough to go home.

Once at home, a nurse and a social worker would visit her. She would continue with medication, and for a time all would be well. Upsets were often caused by things happening that worried Linda. It might be her daughter, or her finances, or her health. Once she began to worry this could build up to one of her episodes. She would stop sleeping and begin to wander the streets again. It was observed that she tended to stay well when she continued to take medication. However as soon as she was well she was always pressing to reduce and then stop it. The nurse who visited her could sometimes persuade her to continue with medication a bit longer but eventually she would come off it. Then a few months later she would relapse. That would be when I would say "If only....."

Because we could not force Linda to continue medication we had to work hard at other measures to reduce her risk of relapses. This meant providing continuing and flexible support. If she started to have one of her worries she might need to see someone every day for weeks on end. She also needed a lot of help to get her to take control of her affairs. When I first met her I asked her something about her housing problem, and her response was "I don't know about that, my social worker deals with things like that." It took years of people working along side her to get her to take back responsibility. Like most people with long term mental health issues, Linda had real and difficult problems. She was very short of money, and the various bureaucracies that dealt with her were generally unhelpful. Linda was seen as having "no insight", in that she did not seem able to understand her problem or to cooperate with treatment. In fact she knew quite a lot about her treatment, but little about the reasons she was supposed to need it. She did not like the drugs she was given, and always said that they caused her to feel bad. She pressed for lower and lower doses - which is one of the strategies that we ended up adopting.

In the end Linda's repeated admissions stopped. They did this because we could not rely on drugs to suppress her symptoms, but had to address the real situation she was facing. She was fortunate that the staff who saw her at home were not put off by the fact that she was not keen on medication. She was lucky that we were not allowed to force her to take medication. If we had been, I doubt whether she would have achieved such a good result. She now only takes medication for short periods when she identifies that she is going through a crisis. She has had one admission in the past four years. It was the result of a real and difficult life event, was quite short, and not very stressful to anyone.

Linda hated being on long term medication. She said it killed the life in her. In order to avoid crisis episodes she was eventually able to devise strategies that did not rely on drugs. There are other people who may be not achieve this. However it was not easy with Linda; it took nearly ten years. It would not have taken so long if good community services had been in place at the start of that time. However the difficult legal arrangements that we were working under meant that there was continuing dialogue about what Linda wanted, and what was wrong with what we were offering. We had to try to give her what she wanted; things such as a good place to live, enough money, help in dealing with the authorities, advice about problems that arose, and people to talk to in a crisis. She even included in her what-could-help list admission to the ward as an option, and some medication in a crisis to "bring her down" and help her to sleep. What she would never accept as helpful was being treated "on a section", and having to stay on medication. We had to accept that she knew more about what her real problems were than we did, and that often the best intervention was exactly what she was asking for. A psychiatry that can impose treatment may not have to listen, and those on whom it is imposed may not be able to speak out.

New legal framework

The new mental health law being discussed will give tribunals an added role. I know that this will be a real problem for myself and my colleagues, and quite stressful for patients. It is intended to establish a culture in which the reasons for detention are out in the open, and subject to regular review. Within a generation the legal arrangements for patients will have changed out of all recognition. We will have moved from a fairly relaxed and informal system to a legal process with all the formality that that involves. I remember the shock felt by psychiatrists when solicitors first began to make regular appearances at tribunals. From then on the law has come to exert an increasing influence. This is not an issue unique to mental health; law is becoming involved in many areas of life that once were left to informal local procedures.

This means that whatever mental health law is introduced, it will be much more rigorously enforced than in the past. There will be more hearings, more legal challenges to doctors' plans. If it comes to pass that decisions about detaining patients are taken by tribunals, (one suggestion), then a new stage in formalising the process will have been reached. This all feels like an irreversible movement, part of the drive for lawyers to take over the world. It will guarantee rights but at the cost of increasing bureaucracy.

I have argued that the pervasiveness of compulsion within mental health services is something that should be faced. The move to formalise all legal procedures will prove very costly for psychiatry. It will involve both patients and staff in a great deal of time consuming bureaucracy. As the same changes are affecting every area of life I do not think there is any way in which the mental health field can avoid them. It is simply a change in how our society does things. It will inevitably make psychiatry more expensive, without direct benefits to patient care. This reinforces the message of this chapter: it is essential that both time and effort are put into finding ways to reduce the need for compulsion, and to reduce its impact. This needs to have a much higher priority than it does now. If a fraction of the effort that goes into testing new, unnecessary drugs went into this, maybe some progress could be made. This may not happen until the rising cost of the bureaucracy of compulsion pushes the subject up the agenda, but that could happen quite soon.

Chapter 16

NEW SERVICES: NEW MODELS

Early Intervention in psychosis (EI)

New services are being introduced which are consciously adopting a recovery model. Early Intervention (EI) is the one of these with which I am most familiar; others are Home Treatment and Assertive Community Care. They have been made the centre of major new investment in mental health services in the UK. They are moving away from the old emphasis on treatment in hospital, and focusing much more on individual problems and needs. Another development in the UK is the Care Programme Approach, designed to put individual recovery plans at the centre of people's care.

I was involved in setting up an Early Intervention team and that brought home to me the cultural shift that is taking place. The extent of the change involved came as a surprise to us, as our initial aim was simply to make sure that people developing psychosis were treated more quickly and effectively. One of the leaders of the EI movement is Prof. Patrick McGorry from Melbourne Australia. He has said, *"ultimately it may be that the early psychosis focus comes to be seen as a Kuhnian paradigm shift."* (McGorry 2000) Why should improving services for people with psychosis have such widespread repercussions?

Early Intervention (EI) is a movement which has gathered momentum rapidly since about 1990. One of the leading figures in the UK is Dr David Shiers. He was working as a GP with no special interest in mental health when his young daughter developed a psychotic illness. He has described the harrowing time that he spent trying to get help. He says that the children's services said that they didn't 'do psychosis', and the adult services said they didn't 'do children'. His experiences gave him the passion to push for the setting up of EI services across the UK. My own interest in EI came from the same direction. I was aware that the treatment of people suffering from psychosis was terrible, and that if psychiatric services couldn't get that right, they were failing in their main task. When I listened to stories of what people experienced when they or someone in their family developed mental illness it made me ashamed to be a psychiatrist. As a clinician responsible for delivering a service, I had to answer people's complaints. I found this very revealing and uncomfortable. (I am talking here about Early Intervention for people who have developed psychotic symptoms. There is a separate strategy for trying to prevent people developing psychosis by treating them before they develop psychotic symptoms in the first place. This confusingly is also called EI. It is an interesting idea but is still at the research stage, and is not what I am talking about. My own view is that there is an enormous job to be done in providing acceptable services for people with obvious mental illness, and that that should be our first priority).

As well as the ethical arguments, the other driving force behind the movement is science. It has been observed that there is often a long interval between the onset of psychotic symptoms and the start of any intervention. This duration of untreated psychosis or DUP was found to be up to two years, and the longer it was, the worse was the long term outcome for the patient. This led to the idea that the psychotic experience is toxic to the brain and the longer it goes on the less chance there is of reversing it. One of the first aims of EI services is therefore to reduce DUP with a view to improving the long term outlook for patients. The hope was nothing less than changing and improving the course of schizophrenia. This is the psychiatric equivalent of trying to find a cure for cancer.

Features of the EI approach

1) Attempts are made to increase awareness of psychosis of the public, community agencies and health professionals. The hope is that this will make people more likely to come forward for help, and that primary care would be more likely to refer them on.

2) Appointments should be convenient, and at a place that is not

itself off-putting and stigmatising.

3) The service should be flexible and user friendly.

4) It is important to make and maintain contact, and for this good quality individual working is essential. People should not be discharged simply because they fail to keep appointments.

5) A style of service is needed that will be acceptable to young people who have had no prior experience of psychiatry. This contrasts with the old 'take it or leave it' attitude of traditional psychiatry.

6) It is important to elicit and explore psychotic symptoms, but making a formal diagnosis is of relatively little importance - except perhaps for government statistical returns.

7) A psychological approach is adopted from the start – a priority being to understand and engage. Psychological treatments are offered for persisting symptoms.

8) Medication is used to treat symptoms, with low dose regimes being widely used.

9) There is an emphasis on sharing information about mental health problems and their treatment.

10) Some of those referred will still be admitted to hospital, some under the Mental Health Act. However it is important that, if this happens, the team remains involved.

11) There is much attention to helping with the practicalities of life including finance, housing and work.

12) Since many of those attending are still involved in education and training, help is needed to work out how to return to these.

13) Cultural sensitivity is important in working with people whose backgrounds are different to most of the workers.

14) Having a worker who has been a user of mental health services can help mutual understanding.

15) There should be a positive stance on each issue, particularly concerning recovery.

This list includes changes to most aspects of traditional psychiatry, separately they are small steps, taken together they amount to a new approach. The medical model is still with us, but with strong attempts to tone down its unacceptably authoritarian style. There is much use of care workers who do not have a medical background, and so are not focused on treatment. In this model psychiatric treatment remains one aspect of the care package, but it should not be the predominant one.

Does EI depend on scientific theories for its justification? The scientists like to claim that it is their findings and theories that are behind the movement. They say that if they can prove that shortening DUP leads to better mental functioning, then the service is scientifically justified. I am not so sure. If it was found that long DUP was not correlated with poor outcome, would that mean we should not intervene early? Should we leave people with the appalling services that David Shiers encountered if the research does not prove the case? I am not convinced the DUP effect is true anyway. Some recent studies have failed to confirm the correlation. It seems some people have psychotic symptoms for a long time without deteriorating, whereas others suffer greatly. I have met a number of people in each category. I think that all these changes to the traditional approach are justified on ethical grounds, whatever the science shows. The joy of the EI approach is that it incorporates many of the non-specific factors that are known to help people; these can be summarised in an individual recovery plan. The justification for wanting to help people to recover is ethical not scientific.

The politics of implementation

Early Intervention has been pushed with evangelic fervour by enthusiasts around the world. One particular way of carrying out EI has come to be seen as the only acceptable option. This involves the setting up of separate specialist teams which can function independently of existing mental health services. These teams require high levels of specialist staff and facilities that are free of old negative psychiatric associations. It is new high profile teams like this that have carried out the research around which the movement has grown. The new EI teams thus have many features of a specific treatment approach: (shades of insulin coma?). They require special training, high levels of staff, a new rationale, and clear water between them and what ordinary teams do.

There are problems and controversies over the introduction of EI teams in the UK. They are new and expensive and need a lot of good staff. There is a real risk that they will poach staff and money away from less glamorous services. There is also the problem that services which are separated into a number of different functional teams are becoming increasingly complicated, fragmented (and expensive.). Once they have finished their time with the EI team, patients will have to move on to 'ordinary' community teams. These are likely to be less well staffed, and still operating with more traditional approaches. Those who move between teams will suffer a reduction in service. The high cost of EI teams has contributed to delays, not only in setting up special teams, but in putting into practice all these simple commonsense measures. This provides ammunition for those who oppose such developments, they can say that they are an expensive luxury that can not be afforded. This follows from the way EI has been presented as a specific, new, complicated service calling for a lot of new investment. It becomes an argument about money, rather than styles of service.

A different option is that EI services should be grafted onto existing generic services (Whitwell 2001). It would have been possible to adapt existing services to take in all the features that are part of the EI approach. I saw this being done very effectively in our small pilot study. The advantage of this approach is that the change of culture that is being introduced comes to involve the whole service.

The problem is that good sensible innovations have been taken over by a powerful pressure group, insisting that there is only one way that EI can be carried out. This way turns out to be very expensive and probably unworkable. In fact there is nothing specific about any of the features of the EI approach that I have listed. It is not rocket science! I think the same principles should apply to anyone needing psychiatric care at any stage. Arguments about EI are like other theoretical disputes in mental health; behind the differing opinions about how people should be helped are professional rivalries. Treating people suffering from psychosis was the central task of medical psychiatry. It is significant that psychologists are playing a leading role in EI, and so are moving in on what used to be a medical monopoly. This may be one reason why setting up new, separate services has been seen as a more attractive option than trying to reform old, failing ones. This gives some insight into the motivation behind the setting up of specific high profile types of treatment. It is a way of staking a claim, and building a professional empire.

The good news is that any enlightened service should be able to implement the features of the new model, whatever sort of team it is or whatever it is called. The biggest obstacles that we found to making changes were in changing our own ideas and expectations. These changes are now moving through the mental health community.

I have been describing how I have learnt about recovery, and how my ideas have changed. I think many others have been going through the same slow and painful process, so that most of what I have described is already well known. However, there are no grounds for complacency. In overstretched acute wards 'naïve psychiatry' is still being practised, and its attitudes are shaping patient care. As one user of services said at a recent conference, "*Mental health workers need to go through their own recovery, acknowledging the need to change attitudes and behaviour.*"

It is a mistake to believe that the answers for personal recovery lie in particular services or models of care. The illusion that we have finally got things right will always turn out to be a mirage. All organisations and structures have life-spans, and the need to reform and develop is continuous. The conflict between what the individual wants and how the state organises services can never be resolved, but has to be worked on. There is a healthy anarchism that is an essential part of being an individual, and it will always seek to escape from institutions. There will always be a role for those who highlight the diseases of organisations, including bossiness, bureaucracy, self-importance and intellectual arrogance. The focus on recovery is a key strategy in the struggle to defend the individual.

Acknowledgements

I would like to thank the many friends and colleagues and patients who have contributed to my slow education in these matters. Working with the team at Marine Hill in Clevedon, N.Somerset was a very happy and productive period. Most of my work was at Southmead Hospital in Bristol where I was lucky to be part of a very positive and supportive team for many years.

References

Argyle M 2001 *The Psychology of Happiness* 2nd Ed. Routledge.

Bebbington P. and Kuipers E. 1994 *The Predictive Utility of Expressed Emotion in Schizophrenia*. Psychological Medicine 24; 707-718

Bentall R 2003 *Madness Explained, Psychosis and Human Nature*. Penguin

Bleuler M 1974 *The Long Term Course of the Schizophrenic Psychoses*. Psychological Medicine 4. 244-254

Bracken and Thomas 2001 *Postpsychiatry, a New Direction for Mental Health*. British Medical Journal 322. 724-727

Brown G. 1978 *The Social Origins of Depression*. Tavistock. London

Brown G et al. 1988 *Life Events, Difficulties and Recovery from Chronic Depression*. British Journal of Psychiatry 152. 487-498

Carr A. 2004 Positive Psychology, *The Science of Happiness and Human Strengths*. Brunner-Routledge

Ciompi L. 1980 *The Natural History of Schizophrenia in the Long Term*. British Journal of Psychiatry 136. 413-420

Coleman. R. 1999 *Recovery - an Alien Concept*. Hansell Publishing

Department of Health 2001, *The Journey to Recovery – the Government's Vision for Mental Health Care*. London. Dept. of Health

189

Deegan P. *Recovery as a Journey of the Heart*. Psychiatric Rehabilitation Journal 19 91-97

Drury M. 1973 *The Danger of Words*. Routledge & Kegan Paul

Eysenck H. 1992 Ch. *Psychotherapy and its Discontents*. Eds Dryden & Feltham Open University Press

Foudraine J. 1974 *Not Made of Wood*. Quartet Books. London

Gelder M. 1991 Ch. *Adolph Meyer and his Influence on British Psychiatry*, 150 years of British Psychiatry. Eds Berrios and Freeman.

Harrison G. et al 2001 *Recovery from Psychotic Illness: 15 & 25 year international follow-up study*. British Journal Of Psychiatry 178, 506-517

Kuhn T. 1962 *The Structure of Scientific Revolutions*. University of Chicago Press.

Laing R.D. 1960 *The Divided Self*. Tavistock Books

Leete E. 1989. *How I Perceive and Manage my Illness*. Schizophrenia Bulletin 8, 605-609

Leff J.P. et al 1982 *A Controlled Trial of Intervention with Families with Schizophrenic Patients*. British Journal of Psychiatry 141; 121-134

Leff J. et al 1992 *The International Pilot Study of Schizophrenia: five year follow-up findings*. Psychol. Med. 22. 131-145

Leigh D. 1961 *The Historical Development of British Psychiatry* Vol.1. Oxford Pergamon Press.

Lodge D. 2002 *Consciousness and the Novel*. Secker and Warburg

Lovejoy M. (1984) *Recovery from Schizophrenia - a Personal Odyssey*. Hospital and Community Psychiatry, 35, 809-812.

Mason et al 1995 *Characteristics of Outcome in Schizophrenia at 13 years.* British Journal of Psychiatry 167. 596-603

Masson J.1989 *Against Therapy.* Collins

McGinn C. 1991 *The Problem of Consciousness.* Basil Blackwell

McGlashan T.H. 1987 *Recovery Style from Mental Illness and Long-term Outcome.* Journal of Nervous and Mental Diseases 175 681-685

McGorry P. 2000 Ch in *Early Intervention in Psychosis.* Ed. Birchwood, Wiley

Monk R. 1991 *Ludwig Wittgenstein, The Duty of Genius.* Vintage

Morgan H.G. & Priest P. 1991 *Suicidal and other unexpected deaths among psychiatric in-patients.* British Journal of Psychiatry 158. 368-374

Parkes M. and Weiss 1983 *Recovery From Bereavement.* Basic Books. New York

Parry-Jones W.1972 *The Trade in Lunacy.* Routledge. London

Pilgrim D. *Psychotherapy and Political Evasions*, Ch in Psychotherapy and its Discontents. OUP

Pitschel W.G. et al 2001 *The effects of family interventions on relapse and rehospitalisation in schizophrenia: a meta-analysis.* Schizophrenia Bulletin, 27: 73-92

Reeves A. 2000 *Creative Journeys of Recovery: a Survivor Perspective.* Ch. in Early Intervention in Psychosis, Ed. Birchwood et al. Wiley.

Roberts G and Holmes J. 1999 *Healing Stories, Narratives of Psychiatry and Psychotherapy.* OUP

Roberts G. & Wolfson P .2004 *The rediscovery of recovery: open to all.* Advances in Psychiatric Treatment Vol.10. p37.

Romme & Escher 1993 *The New Approach, a Dutch Experiment*, in Accepting Voices. London Mind.

Ryle A. 1995 *Cognitive Analytical Therapy, Developments in Theory and Practice*. Wiley.

Sankey A., Hopkins I.K.G., Whitwell D. 1990 *Outcome after Bereavement*. Unpublished paper.

Sargant W. and Slater E. 1964 *Physical Methods of Treatment in Psychiatry*. 4th Edn. E & S Livingstone Ltd.

Sargant W. 1966 British Medical Journal 2. 257-262

Thomas P 1997 *The Dialectics of Schizophrenia*. Free Association Books.

Warner R. 2004 *Recovery from Schizophrenia*. 3rd Edn. Brunner-Routledge

Whitwell D. 1999 *The Myth of Recovery from Mental Illness*. Psychiatric Bulletin 23. 621-622

Whitwell D. 2001 *Early Intervention in Psychosis as a Core Task for General Psychiatry*. Psychiatric Bulletin 25, 146-148

Wilson C .1956 *The Outsider* Gollancz Books

Wright J.H. & Basco M.R. 2002 *Getting Your Life Back: the complete guide to recovery from depression*. Touchstone, Simon & Shuster